Politically Correct Hunting

Politically Correct Hunting

written and illustrated

by

Ken Jacobson

MERRIL PRESS
BELLEVUE, WASHINGTON

First Edition - Second Printing
Published by Merril Press

Typeset in Garamond by Merril Press, Bellevue, Washington.
Cover design and cartoons by Ken Jacobson.

Merril Press is an independent publisher and distributor of
books to the trade, P.O. Box 1682, Bellevue, Washington 98009.
Telephone 425-454-7009. Fax 425-451-3959. E-mail:
books@merrilpress.com. Website: www.merrilpress.com

This book distributed by Merril Press, P.O. Box 1682, Bellevue,
Washington 98009. Additional copies of this quality paper-
back book may be ordered from Merril Press at $14.95 each.
Call 425-454-7009.

LIBRARY OF CONGRESS CATALOGING-IN-PUBLICATION DATA

Jacobson, Ken
    Politically correct hunting / Ken Jacobson.
        p.   cm.
    ISBN   0-936783-14-1
    1. Hunting—Anecdotes. 2. Hunting—Humor. 3 Hunting—
Moral and ethical aspects. I. Title.
    SK33.J23 1995
    799.2'0207—dc20
                                                    95-25140
                                                    CIP

PRINTED IN THE UNITED STATES OF AMERICA

TABLE OF CONTENTS

FOREWORD

Politically Correct Hunting, of course, is an oxymoron. There just isn't any such thing as Politically Correct Hunting, and I'm here to have a good time proving it. Hunters are an underappreciated breed who've gotten used to the P.C. pests and learned to laugh at their pretensions and pretenses. I thought it would be a kick to poke a few holes in the overinflated P.C. worldview and wave a little hunter humor in its face, so I did.

Politically Correct Hunting is the result.

This little book is an eclectic mix of satire, instructions on how to hunt, hunting stories, mockery of anti-hunters, fun, sayings, fact, opinions and observations—all dealing with the issue of preserving hunting. If I make a convert to hunting here and there, that will be gratifying. However, I'm not here to preach but to poke. Fun, that is.

In all the yarns and ridiculous stories I've stuffed into these pages, the point I love to rub P.C. noses into most is this: Everything eats. Life lives off life. Hunters have been around far longer than the P.C. elite, and, like the P.C. elite, by far the most of them weren't human. (Oooo, nasty!) The mavens of political correctness may ignore who and what we are, but hunters are a little more honest.

Hunters have long been fundamental providers. Sure, I've heard all the arguments that hunting is obsolete now that we have modern agriculture and animal husbandry. I don't think so. I think the spirit of hunting is in us all, and is going to stay that way.

Today, hunting is restricted to specific critters called game animals. Only the surplus population of these species is harvested each year. Over ninety percent of each state's Fish and Game Department is funded through sportsman-related dollars—licenses, tags, fees and various taxes. Sportsmen pay for most of our country's wildlife management. Hunting is also a $12.3 billion annual business and a recreation for millions.

The sport of hunting is rapidly being eroded by uninformed individuals and groups who object to it, and have plans to eliminate it entirely in our lifetimes. These people do nothing positive. They put nothing back, they only tear down. They choose not to understand or agree with the need for game management. Their propaganda decries "blood sports" as "killing" and "animal cruelty." They appeal to the emotions of animal lovers in fund-raising appeals to satisfy their personal agendas. They ignore or misrepresent the actual views and actions of hunters. Well, that's worth poking a little humor at, too.

Where did I get all these stories and gags and cartoons? I took to heart the advice contained in Wilson Mizner's aphorism, "When you steal from one author, it's plagiarism. If you steal from many, it's research." This book is well researched.

I am grateful to Alan Gottlieb for his willingness to have Merril Press publish *Politically Correct Hunting*. My thanks to Ron Arnold, who taught me what the phrase "Gawd-damned editor" means while he helped turn my manuscript into this book.

I had a good time putting it together. You have a good time taking it apart.

Ken Jacobson
Liberty Park
Bellevue, Washington

Politically Correct Hunting

ANIMAL RIGHTS ACTIVISTS

I like to keep my enemies in front of me.

A recent government study, *"Report to Congress on Animal Enterprise Terrorism,"* summarizes the activities of the terrorists in the animal rights movement. It says that activity by animal rights extremists has escalated both in frequency and severity in the United States since the early 1980s.

It's a fact that doesn't surprise hunters and sportsmen who have been following the exploits of these self-righteous criminals. According to the study, conducted between 1977 and 1993, the Animal Liberation Front (ALF) and other radical animal rights organizations were documented as having perpetrated 313 individual acts in 28 states against enterprises or individuals using or marketing animals or animal-derived products.

Universities have been primary targets, followed by fur merchants, individuals involved in animal-related business, food production and retail industries.

The United States section of ALF is reported to have approximately 10,000 members. They each deserve a good spanking with their leather belts and a swift kick in their derriere with my leather boot. Their down comforters and feather pillows should be used to tar and feather 'em, they should be denied medication developed with animal testing. They should be required to make full financial restitution and be made to eat wormy apples in prison until they yell, "It's finger licking good," then agree to take their arguments peaceably to the ballot box.

1

For a moment, a lie becomes the truth.

If the animal activists have their way, they'll outlaw rodeos. I don't think they have any idea about the respect the cowboy has for the riding stock of a rodeo or animals in general. I can't imagine any cowboy causing injury or letting any animal suffer.

The bunny huggers have a funny way of looking at wildlife. They really believe that *Catch and Release* (to catch a fish and then turn it loose) disturbs the fish psychologically.

Animal rights extremists are like the cock rooster who thought the sun arose just to hear him crow.

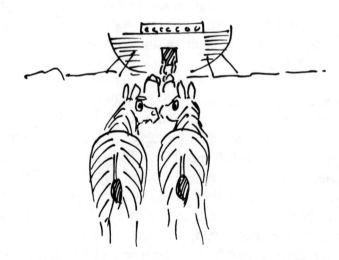

"Now I know why the apes wanted alphabetical order."

You may have heard of the famous rodeo bull by the name of Oscar. Anyone who has followed rodeo seems to know Oscar when I mention his name. I met Oscar in a tavern.

That's right, a big dangerous Brahma bull that had earned a reputation as one of the meanest, most notorious, hard-to-ride rodeo bulls of all time walked into the tavern while I was having a beer.

Each year, for almost twenty years, I'd go to the Brittany National Championships. Many were held in Ardmore, Oklahoma—also famous as the former home of Bonnie and Clyde—now the retirement home for Oscar.

It seems two brothers retired from rodeo about the same time that Oscar was to be put out to pasture, so they bought him and made him a pet. Back in the days when they had ridden Oscar successfully, they made a lot of prize money off him, so they had a special attachment to him.

The brothers own a ranch they call "The Hole in the Wall." A railroad spur runs through the west side of the property and for entertainment, every weekend they have calf-roping competitions in a miniature rodeo ring. Oscar is allowed to roam freely throughout the property like a pet dog. Everyone carries a gun on their hip and the door to the tavern was always open. Actually, it was open because it doesn't have a door. This is a special place.

Warren Montgomery, another Brittany man, and I had been out looking for a place to train our Britts while the National Championship was under way. The National Amateur Championship runs at the conclusion of the Championship. The brothers were kind enough to give us permission to train on their ranch and even told us where we might find a couple coveys. When we returned from our training session to thank them, they were roping calves. We showed an interest, and the next thing we knew, we were invited back the next day for a

Thanksgiving dinner of quail and opossum and a chance to try our hand at roping.

In the meantime, "How about a cold beer?" They pointed to the open door tavern. As Warren and I were having a cold one, in walks Oscar. The bartender saw our startled looks and quickly told us there was no problem, that Oscar was simply there for his daily ration of grain, served in a pile on the pool table. The two guys playing pool just sat down in a nearby booth and drank their beer.

Those events must have spurred Warren's juices, because he went out and won the National Amateur Championship with High Spirit Buck. Each year's winner throws a traditional party the next year, so I wasn't really surprised when I heard that "Buck's" party was going to be held at The Hole in the Wall.

Over a hundred Brittany enthusiasts showed up for one of the best parties ever at the Brittany Nationals. A huge cast iron kettle of chili was served, fired by three propane cylinders. We had heaping amounts of chopped onion and cheese, cornbread and honey, salad, Kentucky While Lightning—the real stuff—cold beer, iced in large buckets, pretty ladies, country music and a new door, "put on special" for "Buck's Party." Everything was there 'cept Oscar. I asked the brother where he was? He told me.

"Oscar done got run over by the railroad tracks."

PETA (People for Eating and Tasting Animals)

To quote those representing PETA (People for the Ethical Treatment of Animals), one of the most radical of the animal rights groups:

"All people should be vegetarians."

"We are opposed to all forms of fishing, hunting and trapping. And we view wildlife management as prey supply management, manipulating wildlife to be offered up for the kill."

"Sport hunting or killing for the sport of it, must be abolished."

"It is a scientific fact that humans don't eat flesh to lead normal, productive lives. The truth is that consumption of meat and dairy products leads the way to death. People eat animals for culinary pleasure, satisfying a selfish desire."

"I just polarized another
PETA person."

Extremists are like sausages.
They are what they stuff themselves with.

John Grady, a top official of the Humane Society of the United States, said, "The Humane Society strongly opposes recreational and sport hunting. It is wrong to hunt and kill animals for these purposes." "The Society accepts traditional and subsistence hunting, so long as it is carefully controlled and does not involve threatened and endangered species." "Little in America could be more cruel than recreational bow hunting. We know that bow hunting causes more crippling, wounding and lost animals that either the shotgun or rifle."

The enemy of my enemy is my friend.

ANIMAL RIGHTS IN THE WORDS OF ITS LEADERS:

Ingrid Newkirk, founder, People for the Ethical Treatment of Animals (PETA):

"Animal liberationists do not separate out the human animal, so there is no rational basis for saying that a human being has special rights. A rat is a pig is a dog is a boy. They're all mammals." (*Vogue*, September, 1989)

"Six million Jews died in concentration camps, but six billion broiler chickens will die this year in slaughterhouses." (*Washington Post*, 1983)

"Humans have grown like a cancer. We're the biggest blight on the face of the earth." (*Reader's Digest*, June, 1990)

"I am not a morose person, but I would rather not be here. I don't have any reverence for life, only for the entities themselves. I would rather see a blank space where I am. This will sound like fruitcake stuff again but at least I wouldn't be harming anything." (*Washington Post*, November 13, 1983)

Probably everything we do is a publicity stunt.... We are not here to gather members, to please, to placate, to make friends. We're here to hold the radical line." (*USA Today*, September 3, 1991)

"Even if animal research resulted in a cure for AIDS, we'd be against it." (*Vogue*, September, 1989)

"Even painless research is fascism, supremacist, because the act of confinement is traumatizing in itself." (*Washington Magazine*, August, 1986)

"It (animal research) is immoral even if it's essential." (*Washington Post*, May 30, 1989)

Pet ownership is an absolutely abysmal situation brought about by human manipulation." (*Washington Magazine*, August, 1986)

"When I hear of anyone walking into a lab and walking out with animals, my heart sings." (To "Market, To Market," *Los Angeles Times Magazine*, March 22, 1992, in which Newkirk condones law-breaking Animal Liberation Front actions and promotes her soon-to-be-published history of the ALF.)

Alex Pacheco, Chairman, People for the Ethical Treatment of Animals:

"We feel that animals have the same rights as a retarded human child." (*New York Times*, January 14, 1989)

Dr. David O. Wiebers, Humane Society of the United States:

"Perhaps the time has come for all of us to recognize that humankind's greatest goal, which outweighs lengthening life through medical advances, is to evolve spiritually.... I see a day ... where all of us begin to come to the realization that it is compassion for all life, rather than scientific advancement, that represents the pinnacle of human existence." (*HSUS News*, Winter, 1992, P. 11)

Dr. Michael Fox, Humane Society of the United States:

(Expressing opposition to use of bug sprays): *"Only a few of the million you kill would have bitten you."* (*Returning to Eden*, Fox publication)

Jeremy Rifkin, *Foundation on Economic Trends:*

"Eating beef is an arcane, anachronistic tradition, a remnant of our past. I predict the beef culture will be over by the end of the 21st century." (*Beyond Beef*, March, 1992)

Tom Regan, "March on Washington," leader and philosophy professor, North Carolina State University:

"It is not larger, cleaner cages that justice demands, but empty cages; not 'traditional' animal agriculture, but the total eradication of these barbarous practices." (*The Philosophy of Animal Rights*, Culture and Animal Foundation)

"Even granting that we (humans) face greater harm that laboratory animals presently endure if ... research on these animals is stopped, the animal rights view will not be satisfied with anything less than total abolition." (*The Case for Animal Rights*, 1983)

"If abandoning animal research means that there are some things we cannot learn, then so be it.... We have no basic right ... not to be harmed by these natural diseases we are heir to." (*The Case for Animal Rights*, 1983)

Regan, when asked which he would save, a dog or a baby, if a boat capsized in the ocean: "If it were a retarded baby and a bright dog, I'd save the dog." (Q&A session following speech, *"Animal Rights, Human Wrongs,"* University of Wisconsin - Madison, October 27, 1989)

Gary Francione, Director of the Rutgers Animal Rights Law Clinic, *The Animals' Voice*, Vol. 4, No. 2, pp. 54-55:

"The theory of animal rights is simply not consistent with the theory of animal welfare or the approaches that reject the rights view and, more importantly, embrace animal exploitation. Animal rights means dramatic social changes for humans and non-humans alike; if our bourgeois values prevent us from accepting those changes, then we have no right to call ourselves advocates of animal rights."

Francione and Regan, "A Movement's Means Creates Its Ends," *Animals Agenda*, January - February, 1992

"As long as humans have rights and non-humans do not, as is the case in the welfarist framework, then non-humans will virtually always lose when their interests conflict with human interests. Thus welfare reforms, by their very nature, can only serve to retard the pace at which animal rights goals are achieved."

"I'll get you, my pretty, and your little dog, too."
The Wicked Witch of the West,
Spoken by Margaret Hamilton in the "Wizard of Oz" (1939)

"It is not in giving life, but in risking life, that man is raised above the animal; that is why superiority has been accorded in humanity not to the sex that brings forth but to that which kills."   Simone de Beauvoir (1908 - 1989)

"Animals feed themselves, men eat;
but only wise men know the art of eating."
Anthelme Brillat-Savarin (1755 - 1826)

"There is no little enemy."
Benjamin Franklin (1706 - 1790)

BACKBONE

Speak softly and carry a big stick.

Theodore Roosevelt has to be the hunter's ultimate hunting hero. He believed in manly virtues, he loved hunting and the strenuous outdoor life. Teddy had vision, intestinal fortitude, and backbone. His mother had schooled him in the chivalrous tradition of her Southern relatives. He was a progressive with an emphasis on duty, a simplistic view of patriotism, and an absolutist understanding of morality, justice and right.

All hunters would be well served to read as much as possible about our twenty-sixth President. He left a legacy of conservation through his actions: expansion of the Forest Reserves and creation of the National Forests and the Forest Service, the proclamation creating the first National Monument at Devil's Tower, Wyoming, and numerous other executive actions. *If he talked about it, he did it!*

It is appalling to see hunters shirk their responsibility to preserve their heritage and sport. It is as fundamental to hunt as it is to work. Today there is not a single organization in the United States that the hunter can turn to that is working to protect the hunters *right* to hunt. Currently, the hunter only has a *privilege* to hunt. That privilege is determined by a number factors: federal and state agencies, various user fees, licenses and tags. Today, there are approximately 14,000,000 hunters over 16 who buy hunting licenses annually. During the past six years we have lost 500,000 licensed hunters and the downward trend continues. We may only have to look at Europe to see hunting's restrictive future.

The *National Rifle Association* is a strong advocate of hunting and provides the hunter *a hunter's lobby*, but the majority of their effort is with the *gun lobby*. They have grown recently with new aggressive leadership to over 3 million

"We need men with less bone in their head and more bone in their back."

members, but only 60 percent of the *NRA* are hunters. The remainder are shooters. The *NRA* has had to focus on protecting our Second Amendment Right to keep and bear arms, a right that some, including the current liberal administration, a number of anti-gun groups and even the U.S. Supreme Court, would modify.

Fortunately, we have the NRA and other national groups fighting for our rights, such as the *Citizens Committee for the Right to Keep and Bear Arms*, the *Second Amendment Foundation* and *Gun Owners of America*, and all the state gun rights organizations. There are also a number of hunter-based groups that do outstanding jobs with regard to specific species management, restoration and habitat enhancement.

Collectively, they make a difference, but most *do not get involved* in the politics of game management. I think they are more comfortable applying their efforts to "on- the-ground" and species related activities. If only they could see that hunting is as much people management as it is resource management and that many major decisions pertaining to hunting are political decisions disguised as biological decisions.

Until the majority of hunters become frightened enough to get involved, to draft and pass legislation, to form strong opinions, join pro-hunter organizations and provide the volunteer grass roots political activism, we will continue to see our sport eroded. All hunters must be registered to vote and then vote for pro-hunter individuals and issues.

"The first requisite of a good citizen in this republic of ours is that he shall be able and willing to pull his own weight."
Teddy Roosevelt, 1902 speech in New York.

"To waste, to destroy, our natural resources, to skin and exhaust the land instead of using it so as to increase its usefulness, will result in undermining in the days of our

children the very prosperity which we ought by right to hand down to them amplified and developed."

Teddy Roosevelt... Message to Congress 1907

Until the inauguration of President Teddy Roosevelt in 1901, our federal government had few wildlife conservation programs. Roosevelt was an avid big game hunter who vigorously supported a new law that banned the interstate shipment of illegally taken game. He established the first national wildlife refuge in 1903. By 1904 he had created 51 wildlife refuges. He more than tripled the national forest system. He was a conservationist before wildlife conservation was the science it is today. He was a man, a hunter and a leader who loved the outdoors and wildlife.

"Now that damned cowboy is President of the United States."

Marcus Alonzo Hanna, 1901, on Roosevelt's accession.

"Turn out the lights."

Teddy Roosevelt... his last words.

BAMBI

Walt Disney is the hunter's worst nightmare.

I wonder if Walt—where ever he may be—knows he is remembered for making the first animal rights movie? When Disney released the classic *Bambi* in 1942, he created what was to become the single biggest deterrent to hunting: *the humanization of animals.* *Bambi* became the symbol of everything that is wholesome in animals, big beautiful eyes, a baby brought into the hunter's cruel "If it hops, it stops" world—hunters who carelessly leave campfires that burn down forests and who shoot aimlessly at anything that moves.

Disney, with his genius for animation, personified animals like never before. He used human voices, music and a strong good-guy/bad-guy theme to bring the forests alive with tension. He made critters lovable. How can anyone shoot Bambi? How can anyone shoot Thumper or Flower, a skunk? What a great concept if you're an animal rights extremist who wants to exploit young minds or old pocketbooks. Humanize all the animals, especially if they're mammals (humans are of course also mammals).

Then, think of all the money you can raise protecting wildlife in the name of animal rights. Anyone who doesn't share your point of view can simply be made a target of ridicule. After all, you're on the side of right. How can killing be good? In the marketing of ideas, images are powerful. Bambi is a great anti-hunter symbol.

It is sad to a hunter to know that there are those who believe hunters actually shoot fawns "like Bambi." It is simply uneducated animal rights propaganda to raise money.

It is all about money.

The wise learn many things from their enemies.

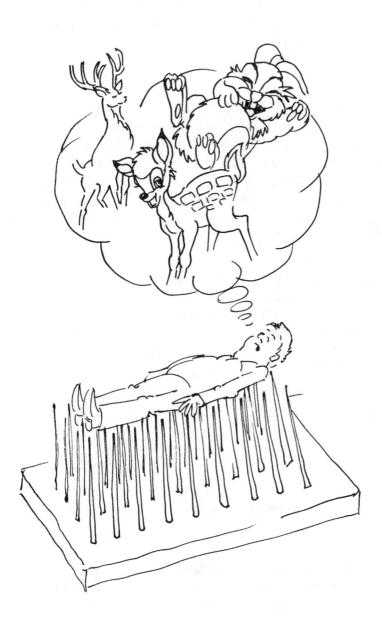

BAMBO

"You probably don't remember me. I'm Bambi's brother Bambo. You may have forgotten what happened to my mother, but I didn't."

Before you look at the results, try to guess what animal you are most likely to be killed by in North America.

You are 1,008 times more likely to be killed by a deer than a grizzly bear. You are 131 times more likely to be killed by a deer than a shark. A vulture actually kills one person every 100 years. I don't know how or by whom these facts were developed, but anyway, for fun, these are the numbers of people killed by critters annually.

Deer	131.00	Leopards (Captive)	.33
Bees	43.00	Jellyfish	.24
Dogs	14.00	Coral Snakes	.20
Rattlesnakes	10.00	Alligators	.17
Spiders	4.00	Grizzly Bears	.13
Sharks	1.00	Cougar	.11
Elephants (Captive)	1.00	Monkeys (Captive)	.05
Scorpions	.67	Stingrays	.05
Rats	.33	Vultures	.01
Goats	.33		

Success is the size of the hole a man leaves after he dies.

Sven and Ollie were driving home from a mule deer hunt in Idaho, when a deer ran in front of their rig and the resulting collision killed them both instantly.

Mom said, "Bambo, you're different."

The next thing they knew, the lifelong hunting partners were standing at the Pearly Gates. St. Pete, who manages the gates, told Sven that he was expecting him, and said "Come on in."

However, Ollie, who was five years younger than Sven, still had some time coming back down on earth if he wanted to return.

"We have had a lot of interest in heaven lately" said St. Pete, "so much that we have had to develop a test to sort out who gets in and who must return to earth until their time comes."

St. Pete went on to explain that the test was two part: the first part "very hard" and second part, "very easy."

Without his hunting partner, Sven, Ollie didn't feel he could return to earth. Together they had enjoyed so many hunts, it wouldn't be the same. They had done it all and seen it all.

Nevertheless, Ollie agreed to take the test.

St. Pete reminded Ollie that the first part of the test was hard, and if he failed he would be returned. Ollie nodded his head in agreement.

"The first question is, "How many seconds in a year?"

Ollie smiled. "That's easy," he said. "There are twelve seconds in a year."

St. Petes' eyebrows raised and he drew back. "That's a very unusual answer. Would you please explain why there are twelve seconds in a year?"

"Simple," said Ollie, "there's the second of January, the second of February, the second of March...."

"Different," replied St. Pete, "but accurate. It looks like you're in. The second question is very easy. Here it is: What is Jesus' father's name?"

Ollie had to think on this one. "That would be Andy."

"Andy," stuttered St. Pete, "How did you come up with Andy?" St. Pete was cautious after the first answer.

"It's in the Bible." said Ollie.

"Well, I'm pretty familiar with the Bible, maybe you can show me where it says Andy is Jesus' fathers name."

Ollie was a little indignant now. Frustrated he said, "It's right there where it says, Andy walks with me, Andy talks with me."

The average man, who does not know what to do with his life, wants another that will last forever.

(A teacher is pointing at a deer at the zoo.)
Teacher: "Johnny, what is that?"
Johnny: "I don't know."
Teacher: "What does your mother call your father?"
Johnny: "Don't tell me that's a louse."

Living causes dying.

"An empty bag cannot stand upright."

Benjamin Franklin (1706 -1790)

"That's the highest shot I've
seen you make."

BLINDS & DECOYS

Sometimes, ya gotta trick 'em.

If I told you, "Today, we are going to see four flocks of Greater Canada Geese by 9:00 am. The first flight will arrive between 8:15, no later than 8:20 and there will be nine birds of which there are two families. One family has four birds and the other has five. We will first see the birds in the sky coming from the Columbia River for the Southwest. The geese will come directly to our field. They'll fly by us to the south, then circle directly to our decoys and blind, with the sun to their backs and land softly into the wind, into an open area in the midst of our decoys," you probably would not believe me.

Yet, that's what Skip had just forecast for the next day's hunt.

I've hunted eastern Washington for over thirty-five years, mostly for upland birds with pointing dogs. I always got in a number of duck and goose hunts, but only in the past ten years, as the chukar hills have become steeper, have I spent as much time in duck and goose blinds. Sitting while hunting is one of my least favorite positions. I much prefer "walkabout" and jump shooting. But, blind hunting can be one of the most effective methods ever invented.

I have a hunting buddy, Skip Coddington, who is the most consummate goose hunter I've ever met. I will admit to you that Skip has taught me most of what I know about field hunting for Canada Geese, but, I wouldn't tell him. He has a huge ego and I don't want it to go to his head.

I'm not as good a goose guide as Skip, mostly because he's the best caller I've ever heard. He's made goose calling an art and claims to have over one-thousand hours of practice. Each year, Skip, his friends and clients kill 400 to 600 big river

"Looks like we're going to have to find another spot."

geese. He won't agree, but I can outshoot him, so I suppose that makes us equal.

As goose guides, Skip and I agree that the real satisfaction is in predicting the situation in advance, not simply sitting in a field, hoping some geese will find us. And, if you're going to take money for a service like guiding, it seems to us that you take the chance out of the hunt, particularly if tips are involved.

Blinds and decoys play an important part in a successful hunt, but decoys in a field the birds aren't using are probably going to be a waste of time. The secret of course, is knowledge gained by scouting.

You have to hunt where they are. It doesn't hurt to have plenty of property, hunting leases and farmers who will give you permission if the birds are using fields not under your control. In today's competitive hunting environment, you almost have to have a professional guide service with all their resources to get a good goose hunt.

You'll get as many opinions about types of field decoys as you will from bird dog owners about their favorite breed.

Eagle Lakes Ranch, Washington State's largest and best duck and goose club—where I guide—prefers the "Big Foot" full-bodied decoy. Eagle Lakes has over 600 Big Foots. We've tried a huge set of 200 or more Big Foots and as few as a dozen. Both have worked. Later in the season birds appear to become decoy wary and shy. Some believe the birds become spooked and are looking for movement.

Real Geese and Outlaw silhouette decoys are both manufactured in Washington. Hunters agree that as birds fly over, the silhouettes appear to move. Outlaw has recently developed a flying goose that really looks like a flying goose. Hunters can use it to attract geese to their decoy set. Then, when the geese start toward your set, you lay the flying geese down and go to work with your call. I've also used garbage bags and rags.

What you use as decoys is usually a matter of cost, convenience and how much you hunt a particular species.

Decoys are also used in antelope, duck, deer, crow, dove and turkey hunting very successfully. Their biggest value is to get the animal into clean killing distances and positions. Coupled with patience and good calling, the results can be excellent.

Blinds vary as much as the game you're pursuing. The most original new goose blind is Skip's "Snow Box," which was developed in eastern Washington for hunting in the snow. Tony Bernsen, Eagle Lakes' head guide, actually had a goose fly into the side of the blind. The "Snow Box" is made of 4 by 8 sheets of styrofoam with viewing ports cut-out and secured with large nails. Styrofoam absorbs light like snow and in some light conditions cannot be seen.

The secret is to make any blind as natural as possible. I like my blinds as hunter-friendly as possible, which means good visibility, comfortable seating and convenient, safe shooting. Placement of the blinds should consider concealment, game location, wind and sun direction

After arguing about whether we should dig in and shoot from the center of the cornfield or from the edge, we set up on a tumbleweed point on the side of a cut cornfield. We dug in the night before and gathered tumbleweed to make five sit-pits for the next morning's hunt. Skip had scouted this particular field for several days. We knew we had a hunt, "guaranteed." Skip hates that word. He's a builder when he's not hunting geese.

The next morning at 8:16, here they come, from the Columbia River, from the southwest: nine big Canada Geese.

The pits were in a line, south to north, with Skip in the number one position to the south. I was in the number three hole. As Skip started his Satchmo routine, (I think the birds would have come even if he hadn't called), the birds flew by to the south to the point where they had the sun at their backs and came directly to our set-up.

Later, Skip would pat himself on the back for such a good job calling. Needless to say, the hunt was perfect. Shortly after, two big birds came in from the south. Skip started calling and they started toward us. They flew outside our set-up to the north, then made a 180 degree circle and came directly back over us. Joe and Bruce had their heads down as Skip yelled "Take 'em."

They were directly over Bruce and Joe, who were in the number four and five positions. When we jumped up, the birds flared, splitting to the left and right. My first thought was to take the bird to the left, but I changed my mind and quickly took the bird to the right. As he started down, I went back to the bird to the left, killing them both.

I still haven't heard the last of that hunt from Skip. To this day, he claims I shot the way I did on purpose.

It's the first time I ever *faked out* another shooter.

"Nice calling, Skip."

All the romance in goose hunting is in the mind of the goose hunter, and in no way is shared by the goose.

Two Southern duck hunters talking:
"M R ducks."
"M R not."
"O S A R, C M B D wings ?"
"L I B, M R ducks."

When you loose your dreams, you loose your mind.
The hunter hunts memories as well as meat.
His memories feed dreams that keep him motivated.

BINOCULARS & OPTICS

A hunting secret is seeing the game first.

Scouting is an exciting part of hunting. It spreads the season. In most states, deer and elk hunting is limited to one or two weeks. Most bow and muzzle loader hunters get a month.

During my travels, I'm always scouting, so I hunt year around. I carry large map books called *Gazetteers* for all the Northwest states. Anytime I see a likely hunting spot or game, I draw a picture of the animals and also note comments from other hunters or landowners. I also find it helpful to jot down addresses and phone numbers for later contact. I am constantly looking for game, to the point I'm surprised I haven't driven off the road.

If I was asked what single secret is there to constantly taking game, I'd say, "hunt where they are." The next most important secret may be "I want to see the animal before it sees me."

Scouting puts you in the best spots. Good optics lets you do the most efficient and effective job of seeing the most country with the least effort. I own the best grade binoculars I can afford. I got a pair of Zeiss 8 x 20B armored binoculars in 1973 prior to a Dall sheep hunt in Alaska. They were selling for about $600 then so I traded a Brittany pup straight across. Best trade I ever made.

I also own a Weatherby spotting scope that I got from Roy Weatherby. I have it wrapped in foam and leather. I probably should get a newer, lighter armored model, but I've got a lot of memories in that scope.

Recently, I acquired a pair of the new Geovid Leica Laser Binoculars. Not only are they incredibly clear and bright, but also by pushing a button twice I can get the exact distance to the object in meters.

Distance brings me to another point. "Make all your shots one-shot kills." Obviously, to do that you have to be very good with your weapon once you do get a chance to use it. You have to have absolute confidence in the ballistics of your rifle and know how far the target is. To perform the task, I prefer a rock solid support and little or no wind.

Wounded game is one of the saddest happenings in hunting. When shooting over one hundred yards, most people fail miserably in judging distance. Yet, I continue to hear stories of kills "over 600 yards," and "I paced it off."

I also have a pair of 10 x 50 Pentax Binoculars that I use for scouting geese. They're on the bulky side, but have proven very effective for scanning the horizon and spotting geese in the air or fields. I also do most of my scouting from my Suburban so I can cover the maximum amount of territory. Without strong optics, I'm sure I would have missed some geese. Usually, you can follow geese in the air from resting waters to the fields they are using. Sometimes they're already there.

My favorite time to spot big game is early morning and late afternoon. Most big game will feed with their heads away from the sun during these periods, which exposes their rears, most of which have white patches. At long distances, this is a distinct advantage. Animals also seem to be feeding and more active during this time period.

I use a spotting scope for two primary reasons, to spot game at long distances and to determine the trophy quality at closer range. Otherwise, I prefer binocs.

Excellent quality optics let me methodically search all the available terrain. I like to get as close as possible to a hunting area without revealing my presence. I have sat in one spot for over eight hours without moving, knowing animals had to be on the hillside across from me. While sheep hunting in Montana, I once looked at a suspicious rock for over four hours before it moved.

Patience is definitely another secret and a virtue in hunting.

There is no substitute for hard hunting and hunting hard.

"I told him to duck!"

BOOTS & SHANKSMARE

If your feet hurt, your whole body hurts.

My first wild sheep hunt was in 1973 in Alaska. I had been reading Jack O'Connor's books on sheep hunting and had got the fever. I talked two hunting buddies, Doug "Fatback" Bison and cousin "Skeets" Osborne, into going with me. It wasn't a hard sale. We were going after full-curl Dall sheep. Some call them white sheep. Gene Needles, our guide and bush pilot out of Eagle River, called them "woolies," a term I still use.

That one trip taught me more about what hunting is really about than any other hunt I've ever been on. It taught me a thing or two about being a "tenderfoot." They say you have to walk in another persons shoes to really understand their point of view.

Gene was a great sheep guide, very quiet and totally dedicated to getting each of us a "full curl" ram. The only time I ever heard him brag was when I told him how good a sheep hunter I thought he was. He countered with, "If you think I'm a good sheep guide, you should see me hunt bear." The bear he was referring to are the "Grizz," Grizzly or Brown Bear, which are the same bear genetically, but are in different geographic areas, the Brown being in closer proximity to salmon rivers.

Once we had committed ourselves and paid our deposits, we had the chore of getting our bodies in shape for the trip. Jack left little doubt as to the rigors we were to encounter. I read everything printed about sheep hunting. I even had a custom rifle made especially for sheep hunting and Alaska. "You may run into bears," I was told.

Ron Marquart, a bird dog man from Tacoma, was also a gunsmith who had built rifles for the United State Olympic Shooting Team. Ron told me he had a special piece of quilted maple that had been passed down to him through two generations of gunsmiths. He had plans to use the blank to build himself a rifle. Maple was hard to work, but still, if I wanted it, he would build me one for this special occasion. We then decided on a Mauser action and a Douglas barrel in 300 Winchester Magnum caliber. Ron styled the shape to resemble a Weatherby. He then fit the stock and grip exactly. To this day, this gun is my single most prized possession. I nicknamed it "Thunder."

For nine months I worked out, I lost over twenty pounds, was tough and was ready to hunt woolies. So, totally prepared, I went to the Seattle downtown Eddie Bauer store to get a couple of last minute things, like a pair of new boots. Those were the days when Eddie Bauer carried real outdoor gear and clothing for hunters and fishermen. Their slogan then was "Expedition Outfitters." Today they are a fashion outfitter, with pretty clothes for the roadhunters.

I bought the finest pair of hiking boots they had, the kind that has vibram soles and stiff leather, "to protect my feet in the rocks." I never put the boots on until we started up the mountain. A half hour later, I would have paid "big hay" for a pound of moleskin. A hour later we crossed a stream, which I stood in, reluctant to leave. That night I took off my bloody socks (that's not a Canadian term). My feet were completely blistered. I wore those boots for the entire trip, standing in creeks every time I got a chance. It was the only low point of the trip. After about a week they felt great, to the point that I later bought another pair for another hunt. That time, however, I broke them in first. It's remarkable how fast you become smart if your feet hurt.

Brains in the head save blisters on the feet.

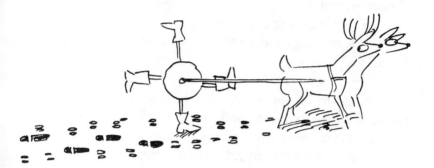

"This will make them think someone's already tracking us."

After flying a Cessna 205 float plane into the Nabesna Glacier area near the Alaska-Yukon border, we set up base camp on a small lake. While Gene flew back for additional provisions, Fatback, Skeets and I went fishing for Pike. We easily caught three to four pounders with red & white daredevil spoons. As we circled the lake shore, carrying our fish, we noticed large scraped areas that looked like bear "digs." On Gene's return he cautioned us not to go fishing without our guns. We had been fishing for three hours already without our guns. That evening, he instructed us to keep loaded weapons with bolts open and "readily available" next to our sleeping bags "just in case."

He told us, "Grizz will first make a hole in the tent by taking a swipe with their paw. Then they'll stick their head through the hole. You'd better be shooting by then." That was the only night I didn't hear anyone snore.

There's a lot of foolish young bush pilots,
but very few foolish old bush pilots.

As we headed up the mountain we had to navigate jangpiles, smaller hills, tundra, and creeks that were shallow from the freezing evening cold that slows the flow, then turns creeks into rivers of rushing torrents in the afternoon as the sun melts the frozen ground. Traveling up creek bottoms is an easy way to climb mountains in the morning. In the afternoon you have to come out on game trails.

As we rested, the question of Grizz and their abundance became a topic of conversation. Gene told us that less than a hundred yards from where we were sitting, a large sow had rushed him the previous fall. I asked if he had shot her. He said, "It wasn't necessary. I could still see her eyes."

He went on the explain that if you can still see their eyes, they're faking and will stop short. But, "If the Grizz's lips are rolled back so that all you can see is his teeth and no eyes, start shooting."

You can cover a great deal of Alaska in books.

I've worn cowboy boots for over thirty five years. They're comfortable. I've even hunted in them, although I prefer a lightweight vibram high top gortex-and-leather combination boot. Fatback has always admired my cowboy boots, so as we talked about footwear for our sheep hunting trip (we have the same size foot), I told him I'd trade him a pair of my boots for his tenny-runners. He told me that they wouldn't help me outrun a bear. I told him I didn't want to outrun the bear, only him.

You are judged by...
> *What you do.*
> *How you look.*
> *What you say, and*
> *How you say it.*

"I thought you shot?"

CALLS

Satchmo and Dr. Doolittle.

In his elk hunting seminars, Jim Zumbo, the hunting editor for Outdoor Life magazine, likes to relate an incident that happened while he was hunting elk with one of his daughters.

Jim, by the way, is the first hunting editor since Jack O'Connor. Outdoor Life could not find a suitable replacement—a tribute to Jack's stature as the premiere hunting writer of his time. It took them twenty odd years to recognize Jim's talent. Zumbo has earned his reputation through hard hunting and great writing with over a thousand articles and a dozen books to his credit. He is also a frequent speaker at a variety of hunting related events, a super-strong advocate of the hunter, as well as a marketer of the Zumbo Cow Elk Call.

While I was serving as executive director for the Oregon Hunter's Association, Jim and I toured Oregon giving Elk and Deer seminars and building membership in OHA. It was on this trip that he told a new elk story. Anyone who has hunted elk in rut knows the value of bull-elk bugling, but only recently have elk hunters learned the power of "cow calling."

Jim was hunting elk with his daughter when a big bull jumped in front of them and dashed away. Quickly, Jim swung his rifle into shooting position ready for a clear, clean shot. As the bull was about to disappear into the timber, Zumbo's daughter yelled, "Use your cow call." Almost startled, Jim called and immediately the bull stopped dead in his tracks.

I have been amazed at the calling discoveries in hunting. New sounds, new methods and new materials. It's probably a combination of "Necessity, the mother of invention,"

"Boy, Skip, you're really good with that call!"

and hunters just plain observing more—or maybe they're just chasing the financial buck.

Most duck hunters know that it is only the hen mallard that makes that distinctive five note hi-ball call, yet out comes a drake call, a low volume raspy quack. I've never used a drake call, but I have heard the drake make the sound and the manufacturer's video says it works great.

I've also been around a lot of hunters who would be better served to put their calls away or like some of my friends say "Put it where the sun don't shine." I don't consider myself a good duck, goose or bull elk caller, but I do a pretty good job on cow elk, turkey, crow, chukar and I make a hell of a squealing rabbit.

I call the good callers "Satchmo" and the poor callers "Dr. Doolittle"—with strong overtones of "Dr. Do-nothing" in my meaning.

I don't care how much a man talks,
as long as he says it in few words.

There was an old owl, lived in an oak,
The more he heard, the less he spoke,
The less he spoke, the more he heard.
Oh, if men were all like that wise old bird.

CAMERAS

It's a damn poor dog that won't wag his own tail.

One does not hunt with a camera. Unless there is a potential kill, a person is not a hunter. Hunting does not exist unless there is a weapon and thinking about the kill. A camera is not a weapon.

If deer painted, there would be many more pictures of deer killing hunters, than hunters killing deer.

Creative people, like inventors, are a curious lot. They never stop inventing. They're like advertising agency creative directors that always have the need to find a better way. I sometimes wonder if creative people are ever satisfied with their end results. The hunt or the process drives their egos to explore and discover and to anticipate.

A favorite Gary Larson cartoon shows two spiders at the bottom of a child's playground slide with their web stretched across the chute, waiting for a kid to come down. One spider tells the other, "If we pull this off, we'll eat like kings."

I don't know many inventors that are eating like kings or hunters who are satisfied with their last hunt. Most can't wait to start planning the next adventure. Every hunt is a new creative venture. However, most creative people do like to show off their latest endeavor, whether it's hunting or inventing. Cameras are an important part of all hunts.

My favorite picture is of my grandson Jared at three and a half years of age on his first hunt with me. Photos have a magical way of rekindling memories. Once lost, they cannot be replaced.

Thunder is impressive,
but it is lightning that does the job.

I like to hunt alone. I can move at my own pace and control my position with regards to sun, wind, stealth and noise. A hunting secret is seeing the game before it sees you, so after I reach the location of the game, I rely on all my "HANK" senses (see Glossary). Over the years, the only shortcoming has been that I didn't have someone to take pictures with me in the frame.

I solved that problem with a new invention I call "Campod." It took over three years and eight thousand dollars to get a US patent. My invention is a simple three wing, two ounce tripod leg adapter that mounts permanently flush to the bottom of any compact 35mm camera that has a self-timer and tripod adapter hole. "Campod" wings swing outward and attach to anything that will serve as ad hoc tripod legs: sticks, golf clubs, ski poles, tent poles, limbs and arrows. It's for outdoor people who want the convenience of a tripod without the weight of tripod legs.

The reward of a thing done well
is to have done it.

If the devil danced in empty pockets,
he'd have a ball in mine.

CAMPS

Build a camp that would make Joe Back proud.

Three things drive us as human hunter-gatherers: All our needs are concentrated around food, shelter and sex. I'd like to add hunting, but that would be cheating and show my personal bias.

The tougher the weather conditions, the more need for a good camp. As a younger hunter I would sleep in the rocks overnight hunting woolies or mountain goats rather than go all that way back to camp, only to have to climb back the next morning.

Today, a comfortable heated motel makes a good camp. I particularly like the hot running water that goes through the camp, those pine bough mattresses and the feather pillows.

If you must make a bull camp, take the time to do it right. If you're going in deep you need horses and equipment and you need to know how to use them right. Wrangling and packing are a real art form that we're losing as fast as our hunting rights.

There was an old boy by the name of Joe Back out of Dubois, Wyoming, who wrote and illustrated a book called *"Horses, Hitches and Rocky Trails."* He died in '86 at the age of 87. Joe Back was cowboy, horse wrangler, outfitter, artist and story teller all his life.

His book is unique and by far the best book on horse wrangling and packing I've ever read. It's one of those books I give as gifts. If you're heading into the mountains or if you pack or are considering packing or even hiring a guide, it'll teach you the right way to camp and the other way.

Thirty years ago, for me setting up camp was just a waste of hunting time. Today, I have become more accustomed to the creature comforts. Yet, I still carry everything I need on my back to stay overnight when I am hunting.

I'd rather have it than have it to get.

"So long partner - Take it easy - Good Luck. And when you come to the end of your rope, tie a knot in it, and hang on."

JOE BACK (1899 -1986)

I made all my money shoeing horses. A dude complained about how much I was charging—$3.00 per shoe.

So I offered him the alternative of one cent for the first nail, then doubling the cost per nail 'til I was finished.

He accepted the alternative. So, four shoes and 32 nails later, he paid me $42,949,672.96.

Yesterday is a cashed check.

One evening before opening day for mule deer in Washington State, Tom, Skeets, Leland and I decided to close up Sammy Castle's Hotel / Tavern in the north eastern town of Republic. We had taken two rigs and earlier in the day had set up camp on Mt. Annie about fifteen miles west. We drank our fill and about 1:00 AM we decided to go back to camp, but Leland needed "one more." Since sunrise was about 6:00, Tom, Skeets and I went back to camp without Leland, who said he'd be along shortly.

The next morning we woke to three inches of fresh snow, but no Leland. We all agreed that he was probably sleeping it off at Sammy's, so we went out hunting and returned at ten. Still no Leland, so into town we went, checked Sammy's Hotel. No Leland. Maybe he had been hurt? Over to the Sheriff's. Yup, Leland wasn't hurt but had spent the night in Republic's Gray Bar Motel.

As we headed back to camp, we asked Leland what had happened. He said he was walking across the street to his rig when a deputy drove up and inquired as to his condition and ability to drive, whereupon Leland stated, "Jail me, (expletive). And he did!"

The thing you need __most__ is the thing you need when you need it.

THE SILENT ALARM CLOCK

If you don't have an alarm clock, getting up in the morning at the right time can be tricky. Many times you simply can't sleep because of the anxiety of over-sleeping.

Here's an old Kenesa Mountain Jacobson Indian trick that you can use if you leave your alarm behind or don't want to wake the camp. With a little practice, you can determine the time you rise within a half hour.

Before going to bed, first relieve yourself, then drink one to four glasses of water. With trial and error — and timing — you can determine how many hours a glass of water takes to travel through your system. You'll sleep comfortably and soundly 'til the time and pressure arrives.

Toilet paper has made many a hunt.

"Sam was born a gun dog."

CLOTHING

If you're going to dress like a road hunter,
hunt from a car.

Ninety five percent of most outdoor direct mail companies inventory is clothing. Talk about choice.

Too many hunters dress to kill rather than dress to go hunting. They would rather look good than be ready to get the job done. Hunterwear is where form and function need to come together. I have a friend that "looks good in the shower," similar to the guy who "talks a good game."

The concept of "hunter apparel" bothers me. It may be great for a football game or a cocktail party or even a Ducks Unlimited banquet. But, if you're serious about your hunting, get serious about what you wear hunting.

In hunting, as in business, I would suggest a 3-step planning process for any enterprise: 1) Goals, 2) Strategy and 3) Allocation of resources. Once I have determined what, where, and when I am going to hunt, I review what I am going to wear to fit the situation. I then do an inventory of what I have and what my needs may be, as well as how deep my pockets are.

I've worn most of the same hunting wear for the past twenty years—with the exception of pants, since my waist size pulsates yearly and may necessitate the purchase of a new pair of jeans. One of my favorite items is a solid red wool Pendleton mackinaw hunting jacket. It has been a perfect field trialing jacket while riding horseback. It has plenty of pockets and a large game pocket that I use to carry a sandwich, apple, camera or candy bar. It's medium to light-weight and repels light rain. It is also quiet when hunting in the brush.

I also have a heavy down coat, a down shirt jacket, and down vests. I prefer a poncho to rain gear but do carry bib style rain pants for real wet conditions. During big game hunts I carry a small day pack that makes a sweat spot on my back. The benefits of the pack far outnumber the discomfort of the wetness. I dress in a layered combination of shirt, vest and jacket for my upper body. Another twenty-five year old favorite is an Eddie Bauer camouflage down jump-suit for cold duck and goose hunts. EB doesn't offer it today, but I understand they do have a darling number in Autumn Leaves Mauve.

Over the years, I found it hard to beat a pair of jeans for durability, comfort and cost. When riding, I wear chaps. They're also great when quail hunting in briars. Some buy custom-fit leather chaps, but I prefer the cheaper adjustable vinyl type. I also highly recommend "tin pants" by Filson. The whole Filson line is great but spendy. I guarantee Filson products will outlive you, and I know I won't be around to fill my guarantee. Also, a good comfortable pair of wool army surplus pants fitted with suspenders is hard to beat for comfort and function.

An overlooked item of hunters clothing is the bandana. It's probably the most versatile item you can carry. If you want to stimulate your creative juices, take out a piece of paper and a pen and list all the things you can do with a bandana while hunting. It will amaze you.

Day in and day out, the baseball hat is probably the best head cover there is. For wet weather, the fisherman's "Sou'wester" is the most functional rainhat ever invented. A number of manufacturers produce good convertible ear flap caps with visors. I'm also a fan of cowboy and Snowy River style hats, except when back packing.

Beware of enterprises that require new clothes.
Clothes make the man. Naked people have little influence in society.

COMPETITION

Never play a man at his own game.

I have a parlor/shell game that I call "Matchsticks." I like to play it because no one can beat me. So far, the only players to beat me are the ones I have taught the game.

To play with matches, form five rows: one match in the first row, two in the second, three in the third, four in the fourth and five in the fifth, to form of a pyramid. The object of the game is make your opponent take a last single match. Alternating turns, you can take one or all from any line.

I'll teach anyone for ten dollars. It cost Ken Sanwick, Jr. three-hundred fifty-four dollars to learn "my game."

Sanwick is the foremost recreational land developer in the Pacific Northwest, a client, and I'm proud to say, a close friend. Among other projects, he created, developed and marketed Sudden Valley in Bellingham, Washington. He is also a chess master. So, when I challenged him to play "Matchsticks," he considered it child's play. We spent an entire evening playing, at one dollar a game. Finally, at 4:00 in the morning, Ken said "Uncle."

The next day, about four in the afternoon, delivery men started unloading fifty pound sacks of dog food in the lobby of my advertising agency offices. He knew how fond of dogs I am. When the sacks had completely blocked the entrance, Ken arrived with two dozen long-stemmed red roses, "For the girls, for any inconvenience," he may have caused them. He couldn't see the girls, so he simply cast the roses, one by one, over the stacked dog food.

Ken is a bad loser, but a "classy" bad loser.

If you are the fastest gun in the West, remember there is always going to be someone faster.

CONSERVATION

White man builds a big fire, then stands way back.
Indian builds a small fire, then gets up close.

There are many lessons of living for us to learn from
the Indian way. But, today's politically correct "man" has a
monumental conceit. He is obsessed with the concept of "bigger is better." Any deviation from the momentum of that
popular societal philosophy lacks both initiative and resolve.

In other words, we must keep up with the Jones, following dutifully in the chains of mortgages, debts and taxes.
All of which are ways for the government and bankers to keep
us under control. Once we marry, have children and assume
the responsibilities that society places upon us, we, in effect,
become slaves to the system. We were never given alternatives
or trained to understand alternative life styles or options. It is
sad our sexual drives overcome discretion and intellect at such
a young time in our lives.

There is another way of living that doesn't revolve
around a college education, Harvard MBA status, banking,
lawyers, Federales or a tax-and-spend government. Man has a
history as a warring creature and a long heritage of lust and
greed. For those who choose the lessons of nature and of the
Indian Way, there is an alternative peaceful family life of living
and understanding nature and man.

Everything effects everything. We have abundant natural
renewable resources that must be managed with consideration
and care. We must bequeath *clean water, clean land, clean air*
and *freedom.* Conservation and a commonsense understanding are our fundamental tools.

Young hunters, in their zest to prove their individual
abilities, may, for a short period, lose sight of what has provided them the opportunity to hunt. For without flora and
fauna there would be nothing to hunt.

We live in a society of laws, a constitution, bill of rights and a federal government and must individually assume the role as stewards of our natural resources by involving ourselves, being knowledgeable and voting.

Hunting in North America is a conservation and management tool of our federal and state wildlife agencies. State by state quotas, limits and seasons are determined to combine recreational opportunities with the harvest of each species. Since 1937, when a sportsman-backed law, *The Pittman-Robertson Act* was adopted, sportsmen have provided the majority of funds for the management of our states wildlife—not just game animals, but all wildlife.

The Indian stands free and unconstrained in Nature, is her inhabitant and not her guest, and wears her easily and gracefully. But, civilized man has the habits of the house. His house is a prison.

"You don't eat a good 'ol pig
all at one time."

Gunvald was a genius. All the city of Oslo was abuzz with his new concept. Many believed it was the closest thing to a perpetual motion machine ever achieved.

Gunvald had just presented his plan to the mayor and city council for zoning approval. The Norwegian Fish and Wildlife Service, at first skeptical, left the council room aghast. They could not comprehend how an average layman, with no biological background could have conceived such a plan.

Gunvald Jacobson was a trapper. His trap line stretched over one-hundred miles. He had made the trip weekly for over twenty years.

An idea that would change his life struck Gunvald one day while skinning a mink. After skinning a mink, he left its carcass on the ground. Then, as he was scraping the hide clean to dry and cure it, he noticed two rats eating the carcass. Such are the elements of discovery.

Gunvald could hardly wait to get home to tell his devoted wife Olga. The next couple days were hell. Gunvald was so excited, he gathered his traps as quickly as possible on his trip home. The first person he told was the local baker. In Oslo, that's like buying a full blast media campaign in the United States. Everyone was so happy for the Jacobsons. Olga was speechless. Finally, after all those years, she would be able to afford one of those fancy new glass scrub-boards, imported from the States.

Gunvald's plan was simple. Mink were in great demand. A single pelt would bring twenty dollars. He was going to own and operate Norway's premier mink farm. He could stay at home, no longer having to take the hundred-mile trips. Olga would be very happy.

The astuteness of Gunvald's plan was that he would farm renewable resources. Since Norway rats are rodents, and extremely prolific, they would multiply rapidly. He would simply feed the rats to the mink, which are also carnivorous. He would have a constant food supply for the mink. When he skinned the mink he would feed the mink carcasses to rats. He would then have a continuous food supply to feed the rats. The plan was foolproof. Others were sure to follow.

Gunvald would surely get the Nobel Peace Prize. Norwegians are so smart.

Many a girl gets a mink the same way a mink does.

Nothing great was ever achieved without enthusiasm.

"Ever make love on a bear skin?"

DIRECTION & MAPS

*It doesn't matter which road you take
if you don't know where you're going.*

Maps should be a way of life if you travel or hunt new areas. Ten, fifteen, twenty years ago, DeLorme Mapping Company of Freeport, Maine, started printing large state map books called *Atlas & Gazetteers*. They have mapped most of the western states. I've found small mistakes, but for the most part they are incredibly accurate and current. I carry them everywhere I go. They're big enough so that I can make notes, record game locations I see or hear about, identify landowners boundaries, phone numbers. But *Gazeteers* are not all I use.

If I am going into new areas, I head first for a map store to get detailed single-sheet maps. To cover remote areas, I sometimes have to special order them. I like contour maps with as much detail as possible: creeks, trails, hidden canyons, out of the way spots that game may seek to avoid humans, places off the beaten path, vantage points to glass. A hunter cannot have too much product knowledge about the land he or she hunts. Maps, scouting and glassing will usually determine if you're "where they are." Once I know exactly where I'm going to hunt I make photocopies for others in my hunt party, then I put my maps in plastic zip lock bags, folded for easy viewing and protection from the elements. While hunting, I also like to mark my path during the hunt and mark any thing special on the map, landmarks, springs, wallows, scrapes, mines, special rock formations, arrowheads, antler drops, heavily traveled game trails and the like. I also like to make mental notes about meadows, dense thickets, vantage points, camp sites and areas that are used as escape terrain.

All animals are creatures of habit and, until disturbed, very predictable. Just imagine yourself as an animal. If you got the hell kicked out of you when you came home at night, how long would you continue to return to that bed? On the other hand if you had been dining, cocktailing and sleeping at the same location for the past month, there's no reason you shouldn't feel comfortable in coming home.

Waterfowling is no different. We don't shoot waterfowl off their resting waters. We can keep more birds in the area for more shooting opportunities in fields and ponds, by establishing no hunting-no spooking zones around special preserves.

If you're an old bull that's been shot at a number of times during past seasons, your survival instincts are stimulated by simple clues: time of the season, doors slamming, gunshots, men talking, the smell of gun oil, camp fires, all signals that increase wariness. The more you know about the game you're hunting, the more you'll appreciate the challenge of the hunt.

"When you come to a fork in the road, take it."

—Yogi Berra

"That compass I got doesn't work."

LOST

Little, orange and white Brittany.
Three-legged bird dog. Has left ear
nearly bitten off. Blind in one eye
and neutered. Answers to "Lucky."

A favorite elk hunting cartoon by "Boots" depicts a soft lady in her hunting garb, standing in a defiantly territorial manner over her recent kill. As a wrangler approaches his downed mule, he calms her by saying, *"Whoa lady, he's your elk, just let me get the saddle off."*

Journey over all the universe in a map
without the expense and fatigue of traveling,
without suffering and the inconveniences of heat,
cold, hunger and thirst.

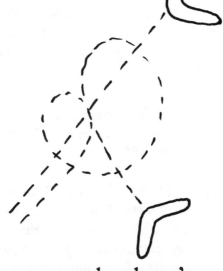

"A boomerang that doesn't come back
is just a stick."

DOGS

Good Bird Dogs aren't for sale.

I've raised and trained bird dogs for over thirty five years, primarily for upland birds and duck hunting. I started with a black lab in the early 'sixties but changed to Brittanies in the mid-sixties. The real reason I choose Britts was to have a family pet in the off-season. The Britt was small, lovable and easily trained. The next thing I knew I was competing in field trials year around. I now needed another Britt, a dog trailer, two horses, a horse trailer, a bigger piece of land, kennels and a new country home to care for the little Brittany.

I became obsessed with developing the finest line of Brittanies in the country. I ended up developing Hall of Fame, National American and Canadian Dual Champion Pacolet Cheyenne Sam. Sam is the only dog to win both the National Championship (field trial) and the National Specialty (show). He also won the International Endurance Shooting Dog Championship, a three hour trial against pointers and setters. That is tantamount to a Welsh pony winning the Kentucky Derby. I also helped develop and owned Ten Time Champion Jacolet Wandering Star and American and Canadian Dual Champion Jacolet Pride.

There was a time that I owned twenty four dogs. So much for a small bird dog. Sam became the foundation of my kennel with a stud fee of $500. I used to tell people I was the most expensive pimp in the Seattle area.

I once ran a full page ad in a gun dog magazine for Sam that appeared next to the National Champion English Pointer Riggins White Knight who was charging a $300 fee.

A good ol' boy from Georgia, "Just had to call me, to make sure that I know the $500 fee must have been a typo."

I explained it wasn't. Brittanies don't get much respect from the long tail folks. Another breeder from South Carolina called and tried to buy Sam. He offered $25,000 in 1972. You can't put a price on your buddy.

"Records live and opinions die."

Delmar Smith, Dog Trainer & Author, Edmond, Oklahoma.

"Sam says there are more quail in that bush than he can shake a stick at."

Field trialing gets in your blood. So, when St. Pete called John to the big field trial grounds in the sky, John arrived to see Jocko waiting for him in the kennel. Jocko was a Hall of Fame Brittany, a National Amateur Champion, a Dual Champion and winner of the National Pheasant Shooting Dog Championship, a win that put the long tailers on notice that a Brittany could compete and win their trial. Next to the kennels stood a big barn, full of hay, a freshly painted cottage with a white picket fence, two big black walking horses, a tightly fenced pasture, a creek running through the back yard and a shiny new horse trailer. Then John looked out the back door and there was the finest looking field trials grounds he had ever laid eyes on. A cock rooster crowed, then a covey of quail flushed near the pond. Yep, this was heaven.

Shortly after, Old Jake arrived, and moved into a similar setting next door. There were his Brittany greats, Sam and Star and his favorite white walking horse Silver, all saddled and setting on go.

It brought a tear to Jake's eye that turned into a twinkle as John came over to greet Jake.

"Saddle up, John, let's have a trial." proclaimed Jake.

"Can't," replied John, *"No judges."*

PACOLET CHEYENNE SAM

(1968 - 1982)
HALL OF FAME
NATIONAL CHAMPION
B.O.B. NATIONAL SPECIALTY
NATIONAL ENDURANCE CHAMPION
UNITED STATES OPEN CHAMPION
NATIONAL PHEASANT CLASSIC
AMERICAN & CANADIAN DUAL CHAMPION

CHEYENNE SAM'S PLACE

There is but one place to bury Sam,
A place were I can find him on point,
A place where he'll come when I call,
A place where he'll always be close...
My heart.

There is only one place to bury your bird dog or your best
friend: that's in your heart.

"Best backing Brittany I ever owned."

DREAMS

You see things and ask why?
I dream things and ask why not?

The hunter hunts memories. You can trace hunting back to the caveman. It was not only a necessity for food, but it was obsessive in every hunters mind. Hunting took up most of the days activities and most of the evenings concerns and conversation, particularly when stomachs were empty. The longer the void the more dreams of success. I doubt that any animal other than man thinks of the act of hunting and the societal description of killing in the same thought. To them, it is simply the necessity of food and survival of the fittest, strongest, quickest or luckiest. Today's hunters hunt less for meat than memories, but the urge is primordial. Memories feed dreams and man must have dreams for motivation.

Hunting is not just a sport, it is a way of life.

I do not know whether I was then a man
    dreaming I was a butterfly,
 or whether I am now a butterfly,
    dreaming I am a man.

The woods were made for the hunter of dreams,
The brooks for the fishers of song;
To the hunters who hunt for the gunless game,
The streams and the woods belong.

Sam Walter Foss, *The Bloodless Sportsman* (1858 - 1911)

I've boiled my life down to
my family, my friends, my memories and my dreams.

ENDANGERED SPECIES

You can't save every robin in the nest.

Ninety-nine percent of all known species are extinct. Extinction is the natural end-point in the evolution of all species of animals. All animals are products of their environments. If the balances of specific species environs change, so will the species. Daily, there are more new species being discovered than are known to becoming extinct—and perhaps even new species evolving before our eyes. Today's threatened or endangered species would be well served to be classified as "game animals" so that hunter-related funds would be made available for study, restoration, management and harvesting.

Humans uniquely have the ability to think and build tools. As a gullible species, we are led to fear what we do not understand and are easily persuaded by the Chicken Little ranting of extremists that yell, "the sky is falling." As humans with monumental conceits and egos, we believe we hold the power to destroy the earth. Anyone who witnessed the devastation and recovery after the 1980 Mt. St. Helens eruption has seen this planet's recuperative powers at work. We may have the power to make living on this planet uncomfortable, but I choose to believe the earth will be here long after our species has become extinct. Our choice is not really a choice at all. We can only spend this flickering moment of life, living each day, one day at a time. Man must live in productive harmony with nature so that both may thrive together while we are here.

Man is a successful animal, that's all.

"Man and animals are merely a passage and channel for food, a tomb for other animals, a haven for the dead of others , a coffer full of corruption."

Leonardo da Vinci (1452 - 1519)

"I majored in hunting
and minored in gathering."

"Descended from apes! My dear, let us hope that it is not true, but if it is, let us pray that it will not become generally known."

Wife of the Bishop of Worcester
after she heard about *The Origin of Species.*

"If we look to long enough periods of time, geology plainly declares that all species have changed; and they have changed in a manner which my theory requires, for they have changed slowly and in a graduated manner."

"As geology plainly proclaims that each land has undergone great physical changes, we might have expected that organic beings would have varied under nature..."

"If there be any variability under nature, it would be an unaccountable fact if natural selection had not come into play."

"Why, if man can by patience select variations most useful to himself, should nature fail in selecting variations useful, under changing conditions of life, to her living products.... I can see no limit to this power, in slowly and beautifully adapting each form to the most complex relations of life."

"Why, it may be asked, have all the most eminent living naturalists and geologists rejected this view of the mutability of species?... The belief that species were immutable productions was almost unavoidable as long as the history of the world was thought to be of short duration... but the chief cause... is that we are always slow in admitting any great change of which we do not see the intermediate steps.... The mind cannot possible grasp the full meaning of the term of a hundred million years; it cannot add up and perceive the full effects of many slight variations, accumulated during an almost infinite number of generations."

"During each of these years, over the whole world, the land and the water have been peopled by hosts of living forms. What an infinite number of generations, which the mind cannot grasp, must have succeeded each other in the long roll of years! Now turn to our richest geological museums, and what a paltry display we behold!"

"This is the grandeur in this view of life," Darwin said. So much so that he referred to it as "the great battle of life."

Quotes selected by Patricia G. Horan in the foreword to the 1979 Gramercy Books edition of Charles Darwin's *The Origin of Species.*, originally published in 1859 and a major book of the nineteenth century. The original edition sold out on the first day of its publication.

Darwin found a plausible mechanism to explain how species can change: by means of natural selection. In the Andes he found marine fossils at 12,000 feet. He discovered woodpeckers in a land with no trees, and geese with webbed feet who never go near the water. Petrels with the habits of Auks. He had stumbled onto the Galapagos Islands, an evolutionary laboratory. In the clear light of his study, he realized he had allowed the land and the creatures and his HANK [History And Natural Knowing—see Glossary] to speak to him — and he listened.

In science, the credit goes to the man who convinces the world, not to the man to whom the idea first occurs.

EROSION

Steel shot and other crippling concepts.

Hunting is our heritage. It is under attack, not only from the animal activist extremists but from those who live in cities and from some in our wildlife departments who advocate an anti-"hooks and bullets" mentality. Many of the individuals who advocate the abolishment of killing, do, however, understand the huge financial considerations connected with wildlife management and recreation. Their only solution is slow methodical erosion.

They would transfer earmarked hunter-related funds from game animal user fees to non-game species and endangered species research. They want the hunters' money, but they don't want the hunter. They seem to have missed the point that sportsmen are the world's largest coalition of wildlife advocates who actually pay their own way.

Collectively, these anti-hunters devise ways to make it harder and more expensive to hunt. They create hurdles, regulations, laws, fees and taxes to make their jobs easier, more important and lucrative. They promote biodiversity and laws like the Endangered Species Act that degrade human importance. They are divisive with claims of imminent extinction of a species to stop industry. They also try to make it politically incorrect to hunt, suggesting that it is uncivilized and cruel to hunt and kill.

Somehow, magically, in the past fifty to one hundred years humans are supposed to have made giant evolutionary strides that have changed who we are. I would remind those who would erode hunting and its heritage that a short six to seven generations ago the Declaration of Independence was signed by our relatives and that evolutionary change normally takes thousands of years—even though evidence of rapid evolutionary change is being discovered.

"Looks like you're going to
rust to death."

Recently, these wonderful politically correct anti-hunting nuts have brought us mandatory hunter orange, mandatory hunter education for seasoned archers, game bird identification requirements, but no efficient methods of training, steel shot that cripples as many birds as it kills, a ban on lead fishing sinkers in Yellowstone, the National Park system, do-nothing do-gooder conservation groups, split seasons, controlled and limited-entry hunts designed to restore dwindling populations that have diminished under the same management that got them to this situation, spike-only hunting, altered opening days, altered opening shooting hours, decoy entrapment programs, reduction of predator control programs, bear and cougar hunting bans with dogs, hunter harassment, and the most creative user fee, license and tax system possible, designed to milk every dollar possible out of the hunter.

I hear Clinton, Gore and Babbitt are concerned with the number of cattle guards in Colorado and are exploring ways to alleviate the problem. They are reviewing their union, funding, training and welfare programs.

Time crumbles things. Everything grows old under the power of time and is forgotten through the lapse of time.

ETHICS

The strongest man in the world is he who stands most alone.

If we didn't have rules, we couldn't cheat. So, when our ethics are challenged, they are questioned based either upon our own personal judgment or what someone else says is morality or law. Is it ethical

- to shoot a duck or a goose on the water?
- to flock shoot?
- to finish off your son's first wounded deer?

If the limit is five ducks, do you turn yourself in for shooting two ducks with a last single shot?

When blood tracking a bull for over four hours, do you shoot a larger bull you happen upon or continue to track the wounded animal?

Do you shoot at a big trophy antelope at 500 yards when you know you've never shot at that range before?

Should you turn your best friend in if you know he filled his wives tag?

If your dog retrieves a pheasant you didn't shoot, what do you do with it?

What do you do if you accidentally shoot a hen pheasant?

If you see someone poaching, do you get involved?

Do you shoot lead when it's only legal to shoot steel?

Ethics are personal. I do not believe that they can be legislated or taught in Hunter Education Classes. Game laws must be obeyed, but when hunting, doing what is right or wrong can be subjective and must be left to the situation at hand. The concept of right and wrong lies solely with role models and parents and the way our children are raised, not at the whim of "womb to tomb" legislators.

IF IT FLYS... IT DIES.

IF IT HOPS... IT STOPS,

Man is the only animal that blushes, or needs to.

As the game warden waded out to check how a hunter was doing, the hunter's chest filled with pride. He had six of the nicest snow geese he had ever shot, and was anxious to show off his kill. He had been hunting in the middle of the Stillaguamish River in Western Washington. He had continuous flights of birds all morning, he knew he was in the heart of the Pacific Flyway. He had also shot well using only a dozen shells. He was lured to this spot after reading an article about the 16- to 17 thousand snow geese that migrate to the Susan Bay area near Stanwood from Siberia in Russia. He had recently moved to Washington from Florida and was ecstatic with the number of birds and his good luck to find such a great hunting spot. He was also surprised that there were no other hunters in the area.

Could the goose hunting be this good in Washington?

The warden asked to see his license, which he proudly displayed, then asked the hunter what he was hunting.

"Snow geese," proclaimed the hunter, proudly displaying the birds white body and black tipped wings.

"Those are seagulls," stated the warden, who proceeded to write the hunter a ticket for $50.00 each seagull, for a total of $300.00.

Later, the warden told some friends that he believed the sincerity of the hunter and might have forgiven him, but the snow goose limit was three birds.

"You quack me up."

"What is moral is what you feel good after,
and what is immoral is what you feel bad after."

Ernest Hemingway

"A sportsman, the Old Man said, is a gentleman first. But a sportsman, basically is a man who kills what he needs or wants for a special reason, but he never kills anything just to kill it. And he tries to preserve the very same thing that he kills a little bit of from time to time. The books call this conservation. It is the same reason we don't shoot that tame covey of quail down to less'n ten birds. I never knew a bad man who was what I'd call a sportsman, he said."

"The Old Man and the Boy," by Robert C. Ruark.

The 10 - 80 - 10 Rule

Statistics show that about ten percent of the U. S. population are avid hunters and ten percent are avid anti-hunters. That leaves eighty percent who do not have strong opinions about sport hunting one way or the other. It is interesting to note that in national surveys the majority of the population is supportive of guns for hunting.

The "Fair Chase" and "Leave No Trace" outdoor ethic we project as hunters may influence the mind and attitude of others concerning the sport of hunting. While I support the ethics of hunting in a moral manner, I am opposed to those who paint hunters as a whole as unethical and would threaten us with the loss of our sport using ethical standards they create. I have never been embarrassed to be a hunter and never will be. And, if I choose to display an animal that I killed on my rig, or on my back or head as a fur or mounted in my home, I will do so, in spite of the political incorrectness of my actions. I will not bow to do-gooders who would determine what is ethical for me.

The Spirit of Fair Chase is an ethic every hunter should live by. Here is a hunter's inventory so you can do a self-test. Ask yourself if you have:

● The skill to use your senses (I include HANK, the seventh sense) with the stealth of a predator hunting food.

● Good knowledge of the animal you're hunting and its habitat.

● An interest in wildlife beyond game animals to the variety of other living things that inhabit the outdoor world, including endangered species.

● Familiarity with your weapon and the skill to make a clean "quick kill." Did you sight your rifle in or practice with your bow?

● What it takes to properly care for the carcass of the game you take and to prepare it as food.

● An understanding and desire to comply with state game laws, wilderness policy, landowner courtesy: "Ask First" and "Leave No Trace" camping and for garbage, "Pack it in, Pack it out."

● The willingness to bring illegal acts before an appropriate law enforcement agency.

Help educate other hunters, especially youth, to the importance of hunting, its heritage and traditions in the "Spirit of Fair Chase."

Beware of those who would ask you to sacrifice, for they would make you the slave and themselves master.

"The Devil is an angel too."

FACTS

Load your brain before you shoot off your mouth.

The next time you find yourself defending the shooting sports, use as much fact as possible to clarify your position.

A recent program by the Federal Cartridge Company outlines some major points that should be memorized.

1) America's *14.1 million hunters* and *6 million target shooters* annually fund more than 75% of the cost of wildlife management in the US through license fees and excise taxes.

2) In 1993 alone, excise taxes paid by hunters and shooters totaled more than *$182 million*, and hunting license fees totaled more than *$492 million*.

3) In 1992, the cumulative economic benefit of the hunting and shooting sports in this country — including everything from trip expenses to land leasing — was estimated to be more than *35 billion dollars* and *680,000 jobs*.

4) Countless groups and individuals deserve recognition for helping to bring many game and non-game wildlife species back from the brink of extinction to healthy populations. And hunters rank right at the top of the list. They've worked hard as individuals, as part of local and national organizations, for well over 100 years now.

5) Here are just a few of the success stories:

<u>Whitetail Deer</u> went from about 500,000 in 1920 to more than *18 million* today.

<u>Wood Ducks</u> went from near extinction in 1915 to the status of the most common waterfowl in the eastern United States today.

<u>North American Elk</u> were down to only about 100,000 in 1920, but today number almost *900,000*.

<u>Pronghorn Antelope</u> now total more than *1,000,000*, up from less than 25,000.

Wild Turkeys numbered about 650,000 in 1900. Now there are around *4,000,000.*

Trumpeter Swans were fewer than 73 in 1935, today their population has reached *17,000.*

American Bald Eagles have soared to the point that they are no longer endangered.

Canada Geese were about 1,000,000 as late as 1940, today they have rebounded to almost pest populations of *3,760,000.*

6) The efforts and contributions of shooting sports enthusiasts in 1994 alone helped buy more than four million acres of wildlife habitat and lease an additional 50 million acres.

7) Nearly 70% of the usage of these habitat areas is for activities other than hunting, such as camping, hiking, bird-watching and nature photography.

8) In the field, and through the legislative process, hunters and shooters work hard to police their own ranks and enforce a strict code of ethics and competency, as well as, educate new ranks of young hunters and shooters for the safe enjoyment of their sports.

9) Many companies do their part as well.

Federal gives generously to many worthy groups, including *Ducks Unlimited, Pheasants Forever, The National Wild Turkey Federation, Whitetails Unlimited, The Rocky Mountain Elk Foundation, The Isaak Walton League of America, the 4H Clubs, the Boy Scouts of America* and others.

We hear so much about threatened or endangered species these days, it's easy to see why some people believe all the wildlife is in trouble, which is simply not the case.

The Council for Wildlife Conservation and Education, Inc. has adopted the term "The Un-endangered Species" which speaks to the success of wildlife management in North America, a term all hunters should be proud of.

FEAR

From Fear to Acceptance

FFₓ FFᴀAA

 The model above demonstrates how we can each overcome fear, whether it is our phobias of snakes, heights, dark-
ness, spiders, computers or speaking in front of a crowd. It
takes us from total fear, (big F), then gradually exposing us to
an understanding of our fears (little F), to a little acceptance
(little A). Then, progressively, to full acceptance (big A), to the
point that we become advocates and even salesmen of our previous fears.

Nothing is so much feared as fear itself.

 I knew sooner or later I was going to run into a rattle-
snake. I had hunted in snake country for over twenty years
and never run into one "mano-a-mano."
 I was hunting pronghorn in New Mexico, near Raton.
It was early in the season and hot. We spent two days scouting
and had located a big buck that we believed would make the
book. I had five-hundred dollars burning a hole in my pocket.
That was the amount of "trophy fee" the outfitter required
should any of the thirty-three hunters who were part of the
trip take a "Boone and Crockett" record antelope. My hunting companion was John "Buzzy" Cook, my taxidermist for
the Seattle area, who had arranged the trip. Buzz had been
told there were eight to ten record animals on private property
that was being opened to hunting for the first time in years.
 The morning of opening day, I was in position at day-
break near a small orchard where we had seen the big buck the

evening before. Buzz took the car and would come in at him from the hills. A half hour after sunrise, I heard Buzzy shoot. Buzz had just stepped out of his rig and peeked over a hill. Directly in front of him was "our" trophy buck. It turned out that this would be the only Boone and Crockett animal taken on the trip. Buzz ended up capeing the other thirty two head over the next three days. Some hunt for Buzzy!

Meanwhile, I was in heaven. Each day I saw five- to six-hundred antelope. We would go to high ground to spot herds, then make a stalk to see if there was a trophy buck. Gradually, most of the hunters started taking non-B&C trophies. I kept holding out, in hopes of the big one. I even started guiding when my guide became disillusioned by my insistence on getting a trophy.

After a while, I forgot all about rattlesnakes. I had spotted a likely big, black-fronted, bachelor buck in a valley and decided to get as close as possible to him to evaluate his horn size. As I quickly crossed a small basin, I ran smack dab into a three-foot rattler. He was coiled and buzzing, ready to eat me. Two more fast paced steps and I would have stepped directly on him. He scared the hell out of me. I jumped straight up and back, all in one motion. I think I defied the laws of physics. My knees went limp and shook. All my fears came together at one time. My first thought was to shoot the snake, but then I figured I might spook the buck. So I just gave the snake a wide circle to get to the antelope.

I had to go down into a shallow dry wash. I couldn't make myself cross it, so I walked almost a half mile out of my way around the draw. The buck wasn't what I was looking for. But it's a stalk I'll never forget.

Since that experience, I've had a number of encounters with rattlers, some unintentionally and some intentionally, and have graduated to a larger "A" in my model.

Lord, if you can't help me, please don't help that snake.

I WANT TO BE ME.

Once upon a time, there was a nonconforming duck who decided not to fly south for the winter.

However, soon the weather turned so cold that he reluctantly started to fly south. In a short time, ice began to form on his wings and he fell to earth in a barnyard, almost frozen.

A cow passed by and crapped on the duck. The duck thought it was the end. But the manure warmed him and defrosted his wings. Warm and happy in the pile, able to breathe, he started to quack.

Just then a large cat came by and hearing the quacking, investigated the sounds. The cat cleared away the manure, found the quacking duck and ate him.

The moral of the story:

    1) Everyone who craps on you is not necessarily your enemy.

    2) Everyone who gets you out of crap is not necessarily your friend.

    3) And if you're warm and happy in a pile of crap, keep your mouth shut.

FIREARMS

When bear hunting, you use a pistol to shoot yourself.

Sven and Ollie had hunted elk in the Ochocos in Central Oregon for years. They had built a relationship with a rancher, Wendell Locke. Wendell has always let courteous hunters who ask and respect the property hunt free. This was Sven and Ollies' tenth trip to the Locke ranch. Each year they would bring a box of Washington apples as a gesture of thanks. Wendell became accustomed to receiving their gift and even looked forward to it. So, while Ollie waited in the rig, Sven grabbed the apples and went to Wendell's front door where he was greeted by Wendell, who was happy to see the box of apples. This year's box contained Fujis, a new exotic apple being grown by many of the Washington farmers. Sven explained this might be the best apple that Ollie and he had ever eaten. Wendell thanked Sven and told them to have a good hunt. As Sven started to leave, Wendell asked Sven if he could "Do me a big favor?"

"Ya, sure, ya betcha." replied Sven.

It seems Wendell had an old mule that had to be put down. The mule had been Wendell's buddy for over thirty years and had packed out over one hundred elk during his lifetime.

"Since you've got your rifles, I'd appreciate it if you'd do it for me."

Sven said he understood and told Wendell he'd take care of it right away.

Sven liked to play practical jokes on Ollie. So, on returning to the rig, Sven flew into a rage.

"Gawd damn Wendell, told us ve couldn't hunt on his property this year. I'm going to shoot his mule." Whereupon Sven grabbed his Model 70 - 300 Winchester Magnum and proceeded toward the corral. Blam!, Blam! The old mule fell over stone dead.

Suddenly, Blam!, Blam!.

Then Ollie yelled, "Run like hell, Sven. I got his horse too."

"Nothing in life is quite so exhilarating as to be shot and miased,

—*Sir Winston Spender Churchill (1874)-1965)*

"I agree you don't know if it's my deer... but we both know it isn't yours."

FREEDOM

The Second Amendment ain't about duck hunting.

"A well regulated Militia, being necessary to the security of a free State, the right of the people to keep and bear Arms, shall not be infringed." SECOND AMENDMENT

The Bill of Rights was drafted in 1789 and ratified by the states two years later. It came as the result of oppressive government conduct. It was written as plainly and simply as possible. *It meant exactly what its framers wanted it to say, no exceptions, limitations, stipulations, conditions or arguments.*

We are the American Republic because of the patriots who fought for our rights to keep and bear arms. As Americans we owe our freedom and liberty to those Minutemen who armed themselves and risked their lives to fight against the tyranny of King George III.

The Second Amendment had extraordinary scrutiny. It was one of 189 original amendments proposed for inclusion as safeguards suggested by concerned statesmen. Thirty-nine of the 55 constitutional delegates voted for the Constitution after 16 months of exhausting debate. Congress approved only 12 of the intended amendments. The states then ratified ten amendments. These ten amendments would serve as the essential rights the Founding Fathers had determined were critical to our freedom and liberty. When the Federal Government was given these fundamental beliefs of freedom, they were given to them as our entrusted keepers, *never to be violated.*

Never wear your best clothes when you go out to fight for truth and freedom.

GAME LAWS

There's good laws and there's bad laws.

On an elk hunting trip in the Gros Ventre Mountains east of Jackson Hole, Wyoming we had a experience that makes a man wonder.

Skeets had shot a two point bull deep in the Gros Ventre. It was hot, so when we arrived at the spot to pack out Skeets' bull, he had already gutted and cut it into five pieces, four quarters and the head. He had wrapped the skinned quarters in cheesecloth to keep the flies off and had hung the meat in the shade to cool. We were all proud of Skeets, because between the four of us he was the only one to fill his tag.

Skeets and I had hunted together for over twenty years when we discovered we're second cousins. Like Skeets says, "You can chose your friends, but you can't choose your relatives."

To save some money, Skeets arranged with a retired hunting guide friend to use his horses and pack gear for our hunt. It still cost us over a thousand dollars each.

The twelve mile pack trip in the heart of mountainous Wyoming was as beautiful as any wilderness setting you can imagine. We were in the land of bighorn sheep, monster mule deer and moose, at the end of elk bugling season.

Each morning, as we saddled up and started out of camp in the dark, we passed a cow moose grazing in a meadow. When we heard a shot one evening from the meadow, we instantly knew someone had shot our camp flower. Through the glasses I could see a hunter gutting her. A hour or so later, he showed up at our camp, told us he had a cow moose tag, and wanted to know if we would help him pack her out? We couldn't believe that he had come in this far, killed an animal as large as a moose and had no way to get it out. Maybe we should have, but we didn't help him. An unprepared hunter is irresponsible and isn't much of a hunter in my book. Three or four fifteen mile trips carrying a load of meat might make a better hunter of him.

When we finally reached the paved highway, we headed into Jackson Hole to clean up and have the meat butchered, frozen and packed in dry ice for the trip back to Seattle. As we rounded a curve we pulled over to a game check station. A game warden dressed in a bright red shirt asked if he could see our licenses and Skeets' bull. He began to examine its hind quarters. We obliged, feeling we'd shortly be on our way.

That's when the shit hit the fan. The warden wanted to know why the scrotum sack was not left attached to a hind quarter? He told Skeets he had disguised the identity of the sex. Skeets pointed to the bull's head with horns and told the warden that it sure looked like a bull to him. The warden told Skeets that the head was not attached and he had no way of determining whether or not the head fit on the four quarters of meat.

About that time, I butted in and told the warden that a five piece puzzle could be put together by a child and that his charge that we had disguised Skeets' trophy was pure bullshit.

There were numerous one liners not designed to win friends or influence the law, but did serve to vent our anger and frustration. We had hunted throughout North America and had never heard of such a regulation. The warden read us the law. He was right and we were wrong. He wrote Skeets a ticket and informed him that he would have to pay a seventy-five dollar fine before we left town. He also told us that he would meet us at the courthouse so that the paperwork could be properly attested.

Our next stop was at the butcher. On our way into town we discussed how we would never hunt again in that "gawdamn Wyoming" and "to hell with them."

"Once we're out of the state they won't have a snowball's chance..."

As we waited in the butcher shop, ready to make our run for the border, who shows up? The warden! He said he was there to make sure we could find the court house.

I've got a great photo of Skeets being led into the court house surrounded by two redshirt wardens (no pun intended). The clerk told Skeets he could protest the fine, but the next court date was sixty days off, which would require the time and cost to fight the charge, and that the state would have to hold the meat as evidence.

I told Skeets "I'd fight the sons-a-bitches." The system is pure extortion.

Skeets is much wiser. He paid the fine.

Some game laws are as crazy as hauling timber into the woods.

Wildlife laws in North America are made at various levels: federal government, state and provincial governments and county, municipal or local government.

Each level of government has been given specific responsibilities. Federal government wildlife laws are concerned with many things such as the management and regulation of wildlife species that are classified as migratory, the regulation of interstate commerce in wildlife, establishing treaties with other countries pertaining to the management of wildlife, endangered species and others.

State and provincial fish and wildlife divisions are concerned with wildlife laws pertaining to the management of wildlife species resident in or found within their boundaries. County, municipal and local wildlife laws usually concern wildlife species found within boundaries of these governments.

"Cousin Al is the one who really has it made. I hear he's hanging in a Wall Street bank."

Each hunter has the responsibility to know the laws governing the hunting of the species he is hunting as well as the laws for the area he is hunting in.

Laws to protect life and property:

(a) It is unlawful to discharge a firearm or cause a projectile from a firearm to pass within 200 yards (180 m) of an occupied building.

(b) No person shall have a loaded firearm in or on a motor vehicle.

(c) Big game hunters using firearms must wear blaze orange.

(d) No person is allowed to shoot along, across or from a highway.

(e) No one shall hunt while impaired by drugs or alcohol.

(f) It is unlawful to hunt waterfowl using a single ball cartridge.

(g) It is unlawful to discharge a firearm from a developed road.

Laws to protect and conserve wildlife

(a) All regulations pertaining to hunting seasons and bag limits are intended for this purpose.

(b) No one shall hunt or molest big game while the animal is swimming.

(c) No one shall hunt in a wildlife or bird sanctuary without a permit to do so.

(d) No one shall hunt using an aircraft.

(e) It is unlawful to buy or sell wildlife, or to keep wildlife in captivity unless a special permit has been obtained.

(f) It is unlawful to release any exotic wildlife to the wild.

(g) No one shall hunt during the hours between one half-hour after sunset and one-half hour before sunrise.

(h) Certain game animals must be registered with the State Conservation Agency so that biological data necessary for wildlife management purposes may be obtained.

Laws governing hunter behavior

The concept of "fair chase" provides the basis for most regulations in this category.

It is unlawful to hunt using:

(I)   poison or drugs
(II)   any fully automatic firearm
(III)   snares, traps or nets
(IV)   vehicles to chase game
(V)   any bait or live decoy
(VI)   recorded or electrical wildlife calls
(VII)   a dog for big game (except cougar, black bear and white-tailed deer in some areas).

Understanding hunting Laws

It is the responsibility of every hunter to know the federal and state laws which apply when hunting.

State Conservation Agencies publish pamphlets called "game regulation summaries" that outline the main regulations governing hunting. This information is updated each year to reflect changes in the law.

Hunters should obtain copies of the summaries and study them before going into the field. If a hunter has questions concerning hunting regulations which are not answered in the summaries, or if any of the information is unclear, he should contact the nearest Conservation officer or wildlife agency office for clarification.

Creating or Changing Laws

Only duly elected legislatures have the legal capacity to create or change laws. However, avenues are available to the public to influence legislation. If you want to see a new law enacted or an existing law changed, you should make your elected representative to the government aware of your thoughts.

If you are convinced the law is wrong, work to change the law, but do not disobey it. Many people have found that as they considered their reasons for wanting a law changed, the purpose behind the law became evident. Studying the law will provide an in-depth understanding of why the law is in place.

A small town that can't support one lawyer can always support two.

Cowboy went to town. Asked to board his horse.
First stable: "That'll be $1.00 and we keep the manure."
Second stable: "That'll be 75 cents and we keep the manure."
Third stable: "That'll be 50 cents."
"What about the manure?"
"What manure?"

"You can't legislate intelligence and common sense into people."

Will Rogers

There is no man so good that if he placed all his actions and thoughts under scrutiny of the laws, he would not deserve hanging ten times in his life.

Yes and No are the oldest and simplest words, yet they require the most thought.

"I was diving on this cute decoy
when all hell broke loose."

GLOSSARY

If it's important, personalize it.

Over the years I have enjoyed creating concepts and names for people, places and things. It personalizes and gives my hunting its own distinctive language. Most are original, but I'm not above stealing good material. Feel free to add these words to your hunting vocabulary. It's not in alphabetical order because I don't hunt in alphabetical order.

Titsup	Dead.
Meats	A hunting buddy who gets the job done.
Soft	A rubenesque lady (the polite version).
Beluga	A white male supremacist with girth.
Girth	The result of copious amounts of fine cuisine.
Luge	An Olympic sport practiced in front of television.
Zone	The area you are hunting in.
Head Green	Mallard Drake
Wandering-Star(s)	A society of outdoors loving bachelors.
Ad Astra Per Aspera	"To the stars through hardships"
Thunderstick	My favorite 3" Browning Auto 5 12ga. shotgun, or
Thunder	My favorite custom 300 Winchester Magnum rifle
Jangpiles	Dead falls and bramble that elk cruise through.
Walkabout	What you do to get out of the blind (or using shanksmare).
Rooster	Cogburn, ring neck pheasants
Cheaters	Chukar that hang back after the covey flushes

Quackers	Ducks
Migratory Quail	Doves
Woolies	Mountain Sheep
Bionics	200 pt. Class V Rocky Mountain Woolies
Gumballed	Stuck in a shitty spot
Snow Box	Skip's styrofoam goose blinds, a/k/a Egg Cartons
Chicken Coop	A field full of geese
Real Fine	Doesn't get any better
Miracle	After I shoot, if something doesn't fall.
Dudes	Hunters who pay.
Flocknockers	Duck and Goose hunters
HANK	History And Natural Knowing, or the seventh sense.
Tips	Something appreciated, never expected.
Skybinders	S.O.B.s that shoot at ducks or geese out of range.
"Take 'em"	What you hear right after "Boom! Boom!"
Dem Duck	What we're huntin' fo.
Super Duck	World's largest decoy to promote DU.
One of One	Raised over $500,000 for DU (Sponsored by Coors). Great project.
Feathers	Wild Turkey on the rocks.
Nectar of the Gods	Aka Wild Turkey.
Same Thing	What you meant to say, but didn't, but was still understood.
Rig	A 4x4 hunting vehicle, suburban, pick-up truck.
Limit	A rare occasion. Same as filling a tag.
Federales	BATF, IRS, CIA, FBI, USF&WS, Fish & Game Departments.
Goose	My brother, love ya bro.
Lead Shot	Something that still works in 410 & 28 gauge shotguns.

Princess	Any pert cute lady.
Young Lady	Something flattering to call any female.
Grandchildren	If I knew they'd be this much fun, I'da had 'em first. J-Boy, Katie & Megan
Scrap Ducks	Anything other than mallards, pintails and cans.
Significant other(s)	Designated other than mallard types.
River birds	Big Canada Geese.
Honks	Big Canada Geese.
Squeakers	Little Canada Geese, hate'em.
Easy birds	Predictable flights, usually early season field geese.
Satchmo	Good with a call / duck, goose, turkey or elk.
Dr. Doolittle	Someone who shouldn't call.
Coatrack	A really good mule deer.
Wally	Wall mount trophy.
Campod	Tripod leg adaptor. Great invention.
Duckdawg	A decoy / duck retriever. Great invention.
Blindside	Great new strategy game. "Easy as checkers, endless as chess."
Mort	Code name.
Trophy Wife	Someone who says, "Why don't you go hunting?"
Work	Something you do between hunts.
Shiney	Clean, sparkles, a woman, bird dog or horse.
Hay Burner	That's a horse.
Knocker	A young bird dog, ready to win.
Grizz	Grizzly / Brown Bear, for his size, meaner than a shrew.
Basalt Grizz	Yellow Belly Marmots.
Sage Rats	Various ground squirrels.
Corkscrew	40 1/4" Trophy Dall Sheep on my fireplace.

Sam	That *one* great bird dog you get once in a lifetime.
Star	That *second* great bird dog you get once in a lifetime.
Jocko	Opened the long-tails' eyes. Johnny Munson's great Brittany.
Silver	The best walking horse I'll ever own.
Yotta	Yotta Know Identification Games.
Testimony	Hurried presentations by non-b i o l o-gists (hunters) to wildlife commissioners who have already made up their minds.
Watash	Rod Eyring, my mentor
Flyboy	Pilot.
Big Hay	Large amount of money.
Wade	A good name for a duck.
Big Guy	God.
Whisky	All forms of inferior alcoholic beverage 'cept Feathers.
Target	A good name for a cat.
Lofting	Spooking or moving birds.
Ballard Mallards	Seagulls (Ballard is a district of Seattle known for its waterfront and Scandihoovian fisherfolk).
Half-timers	Forgetting some of the time.
Candy store	An area full of game.
Jawbone	Talking.
Jabber the hut	Constant jabbering.
Flowers	Camp wildlife, do not shoot.
Wona(s)	Women of Negotiated Affections
McGyver tape	Duct tape
Wet box	shower
Poet	liar
Kenesa Mountain Jacobson	aka Ken Jacobson

GUN CONTROL

There are over 22,000 gun control laws.

Advocates of gun control have always promised a great deal in return for restricting the rights guaranteed in the Constitution. The most important positive effect of gun control, they claim, is that it will reduce the crime rate. Since this claim was first made, there have been a number of studies done on the effects of various types of gun control legislation. The weight of the evidence suggests that gun control has not reduced crime, cannot reduce crime, and, in fact, is very likely to increase crime rates.

The odds of implementing a successful gun control law, one which reduces the rate of violent crime, are indeed slim. David B. Kopel, a policy analyst for the CATO Institute, writes:

> In sum, what benefits would strict gun control yield? The experience of other nations shows that a black market pool of illegal guns will remain available to criminals who want one. In no nation (with strict gun control) except Japan, was obtaining a gun more than a little inconvenient for a criminal. Controls at best, might turn some gun-related murders into knife related murders, or some gun-related robberies into knife related robberies, a rather dubious social benefit. Some researchers suggest that control might reduce domestic homicide, and the main victims of the policy would be battered wives. Gun Control would likely reduce gun suicide, but the evidence from Japan, Britain and Canada suggests that gun-related suicide would simply be replaced by other methods of self-destruction.

"Either Jake's figured out a new way
to shoot those spooky turkeys or he's
given up huntin' 'em."

There is no reason to believe that criminals will obey gun laws any more than they obey robbery, murder, or rape laws. In fact, the majority of criminals already acquire their guns in illegal ways. The Bureau of Justice Statistics reports that in 1991, 73% of state prison inmates who had possessed a gun had acquired a gun by some means other than by purchasing it legally. Theft, purchase on the black market, acquisition from family or friends or through other informal means accounted for those firearms.

Experienced police officers agree that gun control laws are ineffective in reducing gun-related crime. In a 1995 survey of all sheriffs and police chiefs in the U.S., 79.5% did not believe that the passage of the Brady Bill prevented a single criminal from obtaining a firearm in their community.

That armed private citizens are effective in crime reduction has been proven by firearms training programs across the nation. Evidence suggests that when guns in the hands of private citizens are both common and publicized, the crime rate tends to drop. For instance, in Orlando, Florida, in response to concerns about the sharply increasing rape rate, police instituted a heavily publicized firearms training course in which over 2,500 women were trained. In the following year, rape dropped 88% there, although rape rates remained constant in the rest of Florida and in the U.S. When the city council of Kennesaw, Georgia, passed a city ordinance requiring heads of households to have at least one gun in their homes, there immediately followed an 89% decrease in residential burglaries.

It is a fact that most criminals are looking for an easy mark — not someone who will make trouble for them. Fifty-seven percent of convicts agree that "Criminals are more worried about running into an armed victim than they are about running into the police." Forty-three percent said they had, at sometime in their lives, decided not to commit a crime because they knew or believed the potential victim was carrying a gun. Fifty-eight percent agreed that "A store owner who is known to keep a gun on the premises is not going to get robbed very often."

It should be clear that gun control, in any form, is extremely unlikely to be successful in reducing the crime rate, and has no history of success in the United States. Moreover, the evidence suggests that gun control could not be successfully enforced without disregarding the freedoms guaranteed in the Bill of Rights. Gun control has been a failure everywhere it has been tried.

All of us would like to see crime reduced. But we need to be reasonable and practical, not emotional, when we assess the causes of crime. The fact of the matter is, guns do not usually kill people unless people pull the triggers any more than the presence of alcohol makes people alcoholics unless people drink it or the presence of drugs makes people commit suicide unless someone willingly takes an overdose. Ultimately, individuals, not society or some inanimate object, are responsible for what goes on in this world.

"American by birth, gunowner by choice."
—Alan M. Gottlieb

"I think we're going to have to fly higher."

94   **Ken Jacobson**

HABIT & INSTINCT

Don't believe in the concept of the one-man-dog.

The first fundamental in training dogs is understanding that dogs are creatures of habit. We must also differentiate between habits and instincts. It is hard to separate them and discuss one without the other. Using dog training serves as a workshop for understanding other animals as well.

Darwin did lengthy studies on instinct, so much so that he specifically isolated it as subject matter in his book *The Origins of Species*. He was particularly interested in slave-making ants and their (cow) aphids, hive-making bees, birds that lay their eggs in other birds nests (e.g., the cuckoo), the ostrich and parasitic bees. He continually blended habit with instinct to show their close relationship. He stated that natural instincts are lost under domestication and used the domestic chicken to illustrate the point.

"On the other hand, young chickens have lost, wholly by habit, the fear of the dog and cat which no doubt was originally instinctive in them, in the same way as it is so plainly instinctive in young pheasants, though reared under a hen. It is not that chickens have lost all fear, but fear only of dogs and cats, for if the hen gives the danger-chuckle, they will run (more especially young turkeys) from under her, and conceal themselves in the surrounding grass of thickets; and this is evidently done for the instinctive purpose of allowing, as we see in wild ground-birds, their mother to fly away. But this instinct retained by our chickens has become useless under domestication, for the mother-hen has also lost by the disuse the power of flight.

"It may be doubted whether any one would have thought of training a dog to point, had not some one dog naturally shown a tendency in this line; and this is known occasionally to happen, as I once saw in a pure terrier. When the first tendency was once displayed, methodical selection and the inherited effects of compulsory training in each successive generation would soon complete the work, as each man tries to procure, without intending to improve the breed, dogs which will stand and hunt best. On the other hand, habit alone in some cases has sufficed."

He also explained that animal fear of any particular enemy is certainly an instinctive quality - strengthened by experience and time, but the fear of man is slowly acquired.

While hunting in northeastern Montana for pheasant I witnessed a covey of huns literally throw themselves on the ground in cover, directly in front of me. They were as frightened as any animal I have seen, other than man. They were being chased by a red-tailed hawk who was shrieking as he swooped low, missing his prey. I've also hunted deer, antelope and coyote in the wide open spaces, not believing that they had seen me from over a mile away, then had them break into a full run, evading me. I used to set meat scraps outside the goose camp, then sneak around the house through the side door and ambush the unsuspecting magpies. After only *one* time, the magpies were gone on my second attempt when I carelessly opened the screen door. Darwin states that magpies are tame in Norway as is the hooded crow in Egypt. I believe, from my experiences, that the magpie, raven, crow and jays are the most intelligent birds in north America.

The outdoors and nature are so much more than just hunting, but hunting does provide an excuse to learn and explore and discover.

Living is learning

Cannibals have long believed they acquire their enemies' courage and strength by eating them.

There was an experiment using flatworms to determine if learned experiences could be transferred through ingestion. The test began with the release of a genetically identical group of worms in the center of a small table. Around the outside of the table was an electric wire that upon contact would produce a shock that caused the worms to retreat back to the center of the table. The first test group took an average of three attempts at leaving the table, running into the electric wire, then finally returning to the center and remaining there. This group, which had learned about the wire, was then ground up and fed to their genetic brothers in a second group. The second group only required two visits to the wire. Ultimately, the researchers were able to put a glob of worm-fed worms in the center of the table that stayed there and made no attempt to leave.

Scary, huh?

If this worked on people, would we educate the kids by having Professor Teachum over for dinner?

"You can observe a lot just by looking."

Yogi Berra

I once asked Delmar Smith, one of the premier dog trainers in the world, what was the secret to making a bird dog a bird dog? His simple answer was to put the dog down on birds every day, then pick it up after he pointed another bird every day for a year. That's 728 birds pointed in a year. Any hunter would love to own that bird dog.

Nothing is stronger than habit.

HANK

History And Natural Knowing, the seventh sense.

Have you ever looked at a mountain or a brushy draw and absolutely knew that you would find deer there?

Have you ever exchanged eye contact with some special person and felt that the chemistry was instantly right?

Have you ever seen a spot in a creek or river that you just had to throw a fly into for a big rainbow?

I call this state of being HANK — History And Natural Knowing. I believe it is an unidentified *seventh sense* that is the cumulation of all our senses, including our sixth sense.

As humans, we absorb much of our personal knowledge through our senses, environment and exposures. We add to these senses History through participation, reading, television, radio, videos, conversation and other communication media. They may even become mutated, altered or biased by memory, daydreams or dreams. By adding personal experiences, exposure to other individuals and their experiences, trial and error, observation and intuitiveness, we separate ourselves from other animals with our HANK.

Certainly the character of Sherlock Holmes had HANK, nurtured by his incredible powers of observation, deductive reasoning, intellect and attention to detail.

No one can predict the future, but with practice, patience and concentration, an individual can enhance his chances of predictable success and lessen his chance of error.

Hunting is the perfect arena to improve and test your HANK. Guides who have hunted for years in a particular area have a big advantage over others who are new to the area. They are also motivated to succeed because guiding is their vocation, their subsistence. Most of their business comes from referrals and satisfied repeat customers. It is important that they manage the resources at their disposal. They must maintain sustained yields of game for their own personal survival or find a different line of work.

They are continually in pursuit of knowledge of the game in the areas they hunt. They work hard to obtain an advantage, gathering their knowledge from a variety of sources: other hunters, trappers, government workers, the game department and continual scouting. They may even fly their areas. They may find a variety of clues, like dung, scrapes, wallows, tracks, the presence of predators, coyote, cougar or eagles, that act as indicators of game. Add these advantages to their knowledge of the terrain, game trails, watering holes, migration patterns, wintering conditions, browse and grass conditions, natural salt licks, and a lifetime of observation and you start to understand the talent of the professional guide. He also gains from reading, story telling and barbershop conservation with his friend and neighbors. His HANK makes him who he is.

It's not the biggest, swiftest, or smartest, that wins the race, but it is the way to bet.

"My horoscope says I'm going to meet a bearded stranger."

HERITAGE

Cavemen didn't use spears to kill ferns and vegetables.

As a thinking human, man has been a hunter through-out his continuous being. Man is technically an omnivore, "one who can eat everything." Most human groups eat ani-mals or animal products. Meat contains all the amino acids essential to human survival in the form of a complete protein. Individual vegetable products do not contain complete pro-teins. For example, rice contains some amino acids and beans contain others. Separately, they do not provide a complete protein. Together they do. So a vegetarian diet must be care-fully balanced in order to obtain what an animal-based diet easily provides. Also, a small amount of meat provides the same protein nutrition as a large amount of vegetable prod-ucts. The sheer efficiency of an animal-based diet is vastly superior to a vegetarian diet. The optimum diet, of course, contains a balance of all food types.

To obtain animal products, a man must either scav-enge and eat the flesh of dead carrion or the kills of others or he must kill for himself and be a hunter. As the only toolmak-ing animal capable of making weapons, his success over other animals has been great. Mostly man has been the hunter — even though entire civilizations such as parts of India have been totally vegetarian from time immemorial — and mostly man has cooked his meat. It is noteworthy that in the old days the Inuit — Eskimos — ate much of their meat raw and consumed little if any vegetable matter — and that primarily lichens from rocks and berries in season — and led healthy lives. The Inuit had to eat virtually all of each animal they killed in order to obtain complete nutrition, including the internal organs and marrow.

"That's the last time I'm going to tell
you to stop drawing on the walls."

Hunting was also an early form of recreation and to-day may provide a release of man's aggression. Since man is aggressive, he is a natural hunter. We are a social species. We have a social brain designed for species survival. But man has never done very well at getting along with other individuals of his race. As such, we are a warring lot with continual territorial disputes, whether it be over hunting lands, natural resources or ideology.

The shy would not have been proficient hunters. Man's survival as a hunter required an inbred powerful urge for combative behavior.

Through time, man has been a hunter.

There is as much dignity in plowing a field
as there is in writing a poem.

HORSES

Pack it in, pack it out.

Bob was a half hour late.

This was a normally punctual man. Bob Holcomb was the Northwest's premier German Shorthair Shooting Dog trainer. A Holcomb trained dog was broke and a pleasure to hunt over. Bob was of German descent and a disciplinarian. Bob had a system and a work ethic from which he did not vary. When he was working there was little conversation. He had a job to do and he did it. All Holcomb trained dogs pointed and backed staunchly. Every dog was broke to wing and shot and retrieve to hand. It was a system that made over 150 field champions in the US and Canada.

When Bob finally arrived at 7:00 am, forty-five minutes late, he was towing his horse trailer behind his dog wagon, a three-quarter ton rig with 20 dog boxes. He explained that his dog wagon lights didn't work for some reason. He had checked all the fuses and knew he was late. So he had simply hooked up the horse trailer for running and brake lights and got on the road. We were heading to lower British Columbia to run some dogs in a weekend Canadian field trial. Bob had decided not to take the horses because of veterinarian requirements. He had all the health certificates for the dogs, but horse certification was more complicated.

We had a good trial and finished Sam, making him an American and Canadian Dual Champion, one of only a few Brittanies to do so.

As we returned to the border crossing, entering Washington, the inspector asked to see our health certificates for both the dogs and the horses. I was driving, so I gave him the dog certificates and explained that we were hauling the horse trailer empty.

A few minutes later he returned and told us he could not let us come into the US with the horseshit in the trailer. I told him it was American horseshit. He remained steadfast. No horseshit, American or Canadian, was coming into the States from Canada.

We faced a dilemma. We had just been told to go back into Canada and get rid of our cargo. What if the Canadian inspectors were as firm in their determination that we should not bring American horseshit into Canada?

We could be stranded on the border, dog trainers without a country.

We made a U-turn and returned to the Canadian border.

"Why are you coming to Canada?"

"We are here to kick off some American horseshit." Then I told him the whole story.

Fortunately, he smiled and let us go into Canada and kick out our load.

I think Canadians understand foreign relations better than Americans.

It just goes to prove that there are more horse's asses than there are horses.

The best thing for the inside of a man
is the outside of a horse.

Most field trialing these days is from horseback and the favorite breed is the Tennessee Walking horse. During your life you may be lucky to get one great bird dog. Having a great walking horse is a huge bonus.

On a trip back east to the American Brittany Club's Pheasant Classic, I rode my trainers, Rick Smith, big white walking horse named Silver.

Silver had earned a reputation as a great hunting and field trialing horse. While Rick was handling dogs off him, many times Silver would take Rick to the dog, out of sight and on point. Other handlers started complaining that it was actually Silver winning all those championships and not Rick. There's a saying, "More dogs make trainers than trainers make dogs." In this case, a horse, Silver, was making quite a reputation for Rick.

I can't remember why I got a chance to ride Silver, but, the next thing I knew, I was in heaven. The Carpenters' song, "On top of the world," kept running through my head as Silver floated over the ground, easily shifting gears from a slow to a fast walking gait. Well, I fell in love. I had such a case of the "wants," you wouldn't believe.

"Price was no object."

So, after I bought Silver, the greatest hunting horse ever, I asked Rick what Silvers' problems were? It's pretty much a known fact that all dogs and horses have some hole in them.

Rick assured me that he was totally sound, except maybe I might have a problem up in the mountains crossing streams when I take him back to the Northwest. My heart skipped a beat. I was on a roller-coaster. I couldn't take a horse that was water shy back to the Seattle area.

Rick saw my concern and quickly explained that the reason Silver might not want to cross a stream was because he like to fish as much as he likes to hunt.

SIGN AT DUDE RANCH:
For those who love to go fast,
we have horses that go fast.
For those who love to go slow,
we have horses that go slow.
For those who have never ridden,
we have horses that have never been ridden.

HUNTING'S FORMULA

A hunter always kills more flies than game.

$$H = \frac{PS}{EE}$$

Hunting's essence is not succeeding or killing. Hunting should be a challenge, a hunt. It can be illustrated in a formula: H (Hunting) = PS (Personal Satisfaction) over EE (Expended Effort).

Hunting is not supposed to be easy. And most hunting is not. Non-hunters may have the illusion that killing animals is simple. Surely, with the quality of today's hunting weapons, anyone should be able to kill animals. Wrong. I would argue that those who believe that have never hunted.

I once visited an elk-viewing facility near Reedsport, Oregon, constructed by the Oregon Department of Fish & Wildlife (ODF&W). There were no signs that informed the public that hunter-related dollars funded that structure. I overheard a lady say, "I just don't understand how a hunter can stand here and kill one of those beautiful elk." Of course, a hunter couldn't. The viewing area was not built as a shooting platform. She had no idea what it takes to get into shooting position on an elk. She probably doesn't understand the draw system, the fees, the scouting, the preparation and the costs involved in hunting, let alone killing that "beautiful elk." Annual harvest of elk averages between 15 to 17 percent of the total elk tags issued. That success percentage is due in large part to the taking of cows. Cow and doe deer hunts are easier and have more abundant game in most hunting areas. Bull elk ratios of 10 to 15 bulls per hundred are preferred and much lower in many hunts. Occasionally some herds and areas have a 25 to 30 bull ratio. A new popular harvest method of game departments is spike elk hunting only in designated areas. Its purpose is to allow bulls to mature to larger monarch or quality breeding-sized bulls to give better genetic strength to the herds. After the bull ratio increases, the plan is take a limited number of branched bulls under a controlled or drawing hunt. Finding and killing quality (trophy) males of any species requires experience, time and money, as well as the ability to use a weapon.

Personal Satisfaction (PS) is a variable of choice. To a young hunter, any animal may provide satisfaction as a "trophy." The older hunter may have progressed to a more advanced stage, whereby he requires bigger size, bigger horns or antlers, or even "book" status of some the requirements of record books. There is also another type of hunter that could be referred to as a "meat" hunter that prefers younger, more tender animals as food. He is not impressed with the so-called status of the trophy animal.

(EE) Expended Effort is the amount of scouting, planning, preparing, traveling, time and money used in your hunt. (PS) Personal Satisfaction is in direct proportion to the (EE) Effort Expended.

Hunting and shooting can be very different and can have little in common. However, to combine them can be the ultimate hunting experience.

To hunt ducks from a provided blind on a guided hunt is simply shooting. Hunting chukar with pointing dogs that you have trained, that are broke and back, and having the ability to shoot wild flushing birds is supreme.

Hunting from a vehicle is the worst kind of hunting. Hunting off shanksmare is sublime.

When the hunter combines the science of shooting, the art of effort, and the understanding of "HANK," he has reached a level of self satisfaction that only other hunters can recognize and respect.

A man has no ears for that to which experience has given no access.

"How can you brush your teeth in the same water you fart in?"

I have known those who view animal mounts as a sort of status symbol of their manly virtues and will show off someone else's kill as their own. The worst of these is the individual that hangs a head that he did not kill and claims to have killed it himself and tells hunting stories about his accomplishment.

An infamous mule deer hunter was caught for claiming a number of trophy deer he had not shot. His ego must have got so big that he required the additional adulation given him by other deer hunters who know how hard it is to "take" a Boone and Crockett head in a lifetime, let alone annually. A B&C mule deer trophy head is probably the hardest of all North American trophies to come by, unless you buy it.

I saw one of his bogus heads. It was a huge non-typical head, with very distinctive and obvious drop points. A picture of it had been published in two different outdoor magazines some twenty years prior to the hunter claiming he had "taken" the animal. It was also determined that the head had been stolen from a taxidermy shop and the hunter could not produce any kill photographs. It's a sad tale, because this individual had legitimately killed many fine record book mule deer legally and on his own.

A bad beginning makes a bad ending.

A DAY OFF TO GO HUNTING ?

So, you want a day off to go hunting?

Let's take a look at what you're asking for.

There are 365 day per year available for work. There are 52 weeks per year in which you already have two days off per week, leaving 261 days available for work. Since you spend 16 hours each day away from work, you have used up 170 days, leaving only 91 days available to work. You spend 30 minutes each day on coffee breaks that account for 23 days each year, leaving only 68 day available. With your one hour lunch period each day, you have used up another 46 days, leaving only 22 days available for work. You normally spend 2 days per year on sick leave (I think you sneak out to go hunting). This leaves you only 20 days available for work. We are off for 5 holidays per year, so your available working time is down to 15 days. We generously give you 14 days vacation per year, which leaves only 1 day available for work. And I'll be damned if you're going to take that day off just to go hunting.

When I hunt I want to get a bull big enough that I don't have to lie about it.

"You've got worms."

INDIAN SECRETS

The earth is mother.

In 1911 the last survivor of the Yana tribe was found near Orville, California. His name was Ishi. He gave modern man an opportunity to learn the true ways of the Indian. Somehow, Ishi had escaped the ways of white man by living a solitary life in the brushy California hills. His superb hunting skills had preserved his way of life from the encroaching white man.

Today, the annual top Pope and Young award for bowhunters, the Ishi Award, is given in Ishis' name. After his discovery in 1911, Dr. Saxton Pope, the famous bowhunter, was one of the people who cared for Ishi.

Ishi was a relic from the past and became a living exhibition, demonstrating how to make hunting gear, bows, arrows and spears. Then he showed his admirers how to hunt.

An Ishi bow was made from mountain juniper and was about four feet long. Its draw weight was about forty pounds. Its string was sinew from the gut of a deer that Ishi striped with his teeth. He demonstrated his arrow making abilities at the University of California, in San Francisco, where he made points from obsidian or glass with a wooden tool tipped with deer horn.

He described many of his previous hunts, then demonstrated his secret to hunting success. He had great patience and could shoot his bow from any angle accurately. He shot his bow instinctively, although on occasion, he would be very deliberate on a delicate shot. The very nature of bowhunting requires the hunter to be close. His success determines if he eats or goes hungry. Of all the secrets of the Indian ways to hunt, Ishi showed that incredible patience was the most effective method. Ishi could wait motionless for hours, no matter how hot or cold or how worrisome the insects.

The secret of a secret is to know when and how to tell it.

Many of the old hunting techniques used by Indians would be defined as poaching today. They do, however, prove the ingenious mind of man. They may also prove helpful should you ever find yourself in a survival situation. The Indian was not a sportsman, he was a provider. He may have enjoyed hunting, but he took game in the easiest manner possible. He hunted for food, hides and furs. He also hunted at night and is probably responsible for originating many of the poaching techniques use today. The Indian believed that the earth was mother and that all beings were spirits. As such he studied and understood the ways of all animals.

Jacklighting - Many Great Lakes tribes hunted deer by jacking them at night. They would build a fire on a large stone on the bow of their canoe, then place a kind of shield behind it to hide and protect themselves from the glare. A squaw would paddle along the shoreline until they found a deer which would become fascinated by the light and freeze. Most shots were no more than ten yards. For years the white man imitated the Indian. Unfortunately, many still do.

Baiting - The scattering of grain or corn was a common method for getting birds within distance to throw sticks, stones, nets or to shoot with their arrows. When shotguns arrived it was common practice to "ground sluice" whole flocks or coveys on land or water.

Snaring - Sinew, twine and wire were simple devises to place on game paths or at burrows. They were used for birds and game alike. The more observant the hunter, the more effective the trap.

Early Indians had to use natural materials for most of their ingenious traps: rawhide, human and animal hair, roots, branches, twigs and logs. Here are some other tricks:

Bears - Deadfalls were rigged with bait to trip the fall of a log. If the bear could be positioned properly a blow to the head or neck would kill him.

Deer - An effective method was to drive deer into blockades which could be used over and over. Another was the use of nooses attached to a bent sapling. When a feeding animal stuck its head through the noose, it would spring the sapling and would strangle the animal as the noose tightened.

Wolves - Pits were used with revolving doors. Bait was attached to one end of the door that would open when the wolf's weight got on it, dropping it into the pit. Smaller scale pits worked as well for coyote and fox. The Blackfoot Indians also would build circular pits but would line the edge with stakes driven in the ground at forty-five degree angles. They would then bait the trap with deer or buffalo carcasses. When the wolves jumped into the pit they could not jump out. Eskimos used a cruel method that involved the warming and bending of a whale bone sharpened at both ends. It would then be folded and inserted into a piece of frozen blubber. Wolves would gulp the whole piece. When the blubber warmed the bone would spring apart impaling the animal's stomach and killing it.

Birds - Larger birds like the eagle, hawks, vultures and turkeys were trapped with nooses made of horse hair. Their feathers were prized possessions and were required for the making of arrows. Smaller birds and rodents were snared with multiple loops hung from a stick close to the ground.

Quail - By watching their habits, Indians could place small nooses in runways, as well as bait to direct the birds.

Turkeys - Two sticks are driven into the ground about ten feet apart. Another smaller stick is tied to the two sticks about fourteen inches high and parallel to the ground. Observing the habits of the turkeys, Indians anticipated the direction the turkey would come. They then baited beneath the bar and six inches on the far side. They knew that a wild turkey does not seem to be able to withdraw its head from under a horizontal pole. When the turkey was in position the hidden hunters would rush out and grab the self-trapped wild turkeys.

Geese - A goose trench is dug fifteen feet long and eighteen inches deep. The trench is fourteen inches wide. The area is then baited with corn, with a small amount on the ground and larger amounts in the trench. When a couple of geese go into the trench, the hunters run from cover and grab the geese which cannot fly because they do not have room to open their wings.

Crows - hunters would get in trees and camouflage themselves, then hand meat as bait on a nearby branch. Then they would grab the crows by their legs.

Waterfowl - The Woodland Indians would weave decoy baskets to wear on their heads as they swam toward waterfowl. A piece of thong connected the sides of the basket so the hunter could hold his "Trojan horse" basket in his teeth and free his hands to grab the unsuspecting birds.

A well-spent day brings happy sleep, so life well used brings happy death.

INNOVATION

Innovate, never pioneer.
There are too many pioneers with arrows in their backs.

Around 1900 the U. S. Patent Office said there were over 1,000,000 patents and that everything had been patented. Today, there are over 5,000,000 patents. I recently received a utility patent for "Campod"™, number 5,360,194.

Most patents are not totally original, most are innovations and/or improvements to existing products. Most concepts are not original and, frankly, few pioneers ever benefit from their personal or "first" discovery. Most artists seem to be discovered after they are dead. However, man is incredibly creative. I really believe that if man can envision something, he can accomplish it. Our ego is so large that we do not accept that something is impossible.

The more I learn the less I know.

Three hunters were sitting around a campfire after a hard day's hunt, looking and wondering at the stars and watching satellites roll and flicker as they criss-crossed the heavens.

Old Joe broke the silence:

"The twentieth century has really been something. There really has been an industrial revolution. All those inventions have really changed the way we live. My folks came from Montana and I can remember when we first got plumbing. I spent many a cold outing on the two-holer. Yeh, modern technology is really something. What do you guys think has been the most important development in this century?

Slim answered first. "It's got to be the airplane, the jet. Yep, it's opened up the world to travel and commerce. I'd say the airplane. We're in the transportation age. What do you think Joe?"

"Yeah, I like the jet too, but my vote would go for the computer, during the past twenty years in particular. Personal computers are now in thirty percent of our homes. We're in the information age. I'd go with the computer. That leaves you, Smokey. What do you think is the most important invention in this century?"

Smokey thought a moment, then said, "Its got to be the thermos bottle."

Both Joe and Slim said almost at the same time, "The thermos bottle?"

"Yeah," explained Smokey, "it keeps hot things hot, and cold things cold. How do it know? How do it know?"

Of course you can catch more flies with honey than you can with vinegar, but who wants flies?

Hunters have a lot of time to dream and to daydream. During the past fifty years they've come up with an amazing variety of innovations to benefit their favorite pastime.

Following are some of the advancements and creative problem solving products that are widely used by hunters.

> Gore-tex Material
> Thinsulate Material
> Vibram Soles
> Electric Socks & Gloves
> Electric Boot & Wader Dryer
> Pocket Sized 35mm Cameras
> Campod Tripod Leg Adaptor
> Polypropylene Socks, Underwear
> Neoprene Waders, Gloves
> Camouflage Wool, Fleece, Cloth

Face Masks
Compound Bows Sights, Releases, Quivers
Laser Sights
Arrows, Carbon, Aluminum
Broadhead Remover
Three-D Animal Targets
Tree Stands
Game Trail Monitors
Night Time Reflective Gels
Ultra Violet Killer Solution
Game Scents
Game Feeders
Deer Calls
Cow Calls
Self Inflating Mattress
Ballistic Cloth
ATV
Distance Finding Binoculars
Portable Blinds Cloth, Styrofoam, Fiberglass
Electronic Ears
Two-way Radios
Global Positioning Systems
Flying Decoys
Live Action Decoys
Duckdawg Duck & Decoy Pocket Retriever
Waterfowl Calls
Sportsman Multi-Tool
Electric Dog Training Collars
Gun Chokes
Collapsible Shooting Sticks
Recoil Systems
Portable Chronograph
Tracer Shotgun Shells
Polarized Glasses

These are some innovations that have improved hunting. The next time you run into a problem, learn as much as possible about the situation, then consider your creative options to solve the problem. In marketing terms this is called "gap analysis," where you look for new opportunities. Who knows, you may come up with an idea that you can patent and get rich. Then you'd be able to quit your job and go hunting all the time.

Here's an interesting problem.

How would you solve it?

While playing ping pong, the ball went down a floor drain. The ball was floating about three feet down in the 2" wide drain. How would you get it out?

Of all the answers I've heard, the simplest is to fill the drain to let the ball float to the surface. But could the extra water act like the flushing action in your toilet and flush the ball down? Trial and error are part of the innovative problem solving process.

Coal is portable climate.

Rod -   "Jake, I don't know how you make it.
        How do you spend your paycheck?"
Jake - "35% on the house; 25% on clothing;
        40% on Food; 15% on the car and 15% on hunting."
Rod -   "That's 130%!"
Jake - "Right."

I'd rather have it than have it to get.

KILLING

Killing is only 1% of the hunting experience.

If a person has an objection to killing *anything*, I can respect that opinion. And I can treat it as a serious matter. If they are simply using the negative concept of killing as a rallying point around their particular agenda as they eat their Big Mac, then I think they are hypocrites. So, before I go too far I want to set the record straight and define how I see killing as it relates to hunting. This book is meant to be a combination of education, fun, entertainment and observation with the purpose of defending hunting as tradition and an integral part of the human condition.

I hunt because I truly enjoy everything connected with hunting. I enjoy fishing for the same reasons. I take great offense at those who refuse to understand why I hunt and fish and would try to demean me or to deprive me and other sportsmen of what I refer to as an *outdoor way of life*. Unfortunately, there are not many ways to *catch and release* in hunting. Hunting does include killing, as does most fishing. Killing can be an integral and important part of the hunt. It can be that final touch, like tying a bow on a ribbon that finishes off a package. It may also *not occur* at all on a very successful hunt.

I have incredible respect for the prey I hunt. Over the years I've enjoyed learning, observing and watching species being restored by the efforts of our game departments and sportsmen. I've enjoyed it as much as some of my hunts. Today I trophy-hunt for North American big game, which means I usually don't kill many animals. I've had my share of successes and now have moved to another level that defines trophy hunting for me. Many hunters consider any kill a trophy. I can understand that point of view, especially if it's their first kill. In most states the process of drawing a tag for a trophy animal, or even seeing one, has the odds stacked against the hunter.

There are, however, opportunities to buy special tags that increase the individual's chances to kill a trophy. Recently a Montana Rocky Mountain Bighorn sheep tag sold for $310,000 at a FNAWS (Foundation for North American Wild Sheep) auction. That beat the previous year's record Big Horn auction tag of $304,000. The good part of these contributions is that all the funds go directly back into the continued restoration of wild sheep. The bad part, of course, is that John Doe hunters like me can't participate.

The animal world has much to teach us, but I draw the line when animals are given human qualities to bias and twist opinions of uneducated individuals and children against the sport of hunting. I feel no remorse or guilt for the animals I have killed. On the contrary, I herald their lives by photographing and mounting their heads and bodies and displaying them in my home as a tribute to their lives and to my hunting memories. I am neither ashamed nor embarrassed to do so, nor to speak loudly in a crowd about the importance of hunting, its time-honored heritage and traditions, or of the role the hunter and sportsmen have played in the restoration of our huntable wildlife. I will not allow animal activists or environmental extremists to brow-beat, slander or criticize me or other hunters for the act of killing.

One kills to have hunted, not hunts to kill.

LAND OWNERSHIP

*Pay the private land owner for his stewardship
of our wildlife.*

Today the conflict between the hunter and landowner
continues as the hunter looks for more hunting opportunities
on private land and the land owner tries to make a living on
his land while providing habitat for wildlife. A few so called
hunters have made it hard for the courteous and respectful
hunter.

We are the product of earth, a family of earthlings that
are specialists, exquisitely adapted to our environment.

People are primarily interested in other people, yet we
have never done very well at getting along with each other.
Lust, greed and fear have proven to be great motivators. The
grass always appears greener on our neighbor's land. And so it
is with the hunter's view of private property. The private land
owners counter by territorially posting their property and land
leases claiming that they provide habitat and forage for the
public's wildlife. They feel that the hunter is inconsiderate.

With rapidly diminishing habitat, I believe the time
has come for the land owner to be compensated for providing
habitat and hunting opportunities on his land. I would recommend the following way to pay the landowner: a 1X factor
for habitat and a 2X factor for hunter access. The payment
could be funded by tax reduction incentives for the land owner.
This would provide a needed compromise for habitat and its
maintenance, and better relations between the hunter and landowner.

Gone are the days of a man's word and a handshake.
Recently I read a poem written in 1926 by Floyd M. Pyle. Floyd
hung it on the door of his Ellison Creek ranch house near
Payson, Arizona.

I would like to have met this man.

NOTICE

Here's a message to all neighbors,
    all travelers and tramps.
When you're coming through this country,
    and come upon this camp.
Just make yourself at home, friends,
    if I am not about.
The door may not be open,
    but the latch string's always out.
You'll find bacon, beans and coffee,
    milk, and butter on the shelf.
So, don't leave this place hungry,
    just pitch in and help yourself.
You may have to carry water
    or cut a little wood.
But, the ax is in the woodpile
    and the creek is running good.
There's hay out in the stable;
    you can find your horse a bite.
There's a bed for you to sleep in
    if you want to stay the night.
But, there's one thing I will say, Boys,
    when you're ready to pull out.
There's a lot of junk around here
    I'd hate like hell to do without.
There are bedrolls, tents and blankets,
    there are cartridges and guns,
And a lot of things here in my charge
    that belong to native sons.
So, when you ride away, Boys,
    just use a little sense.
For I've never locked this cabin,
    and I don't want to commence.

MEN & WOMEN

I was educated as a hunter and cross trained as a gatherer.

Man was originally the hunter and woman was the gatherer. I have yet to find a reference to a woman portrayed as a hunter until Biblical times. None of the great cave paintings of Western Europe shows a woman hunting the magnificently rendered animals, but they do show men. The little carved images of women found in these caves appear to be fertility figures of some type, not huntresses.

Certainly women were not unable to hunt or kill. In ancient Greek religion, Artemis was the *goddess* of wild animals and the hunt—and of vegetation, chastity and childbirth. The Romans seem to have lifted Artemis directly from the Greeks and transformed her into their own goddess Diana—she was the favorite goddess in Roman rural areas. In India, long before Biblical times, Kali was worshipped as the goddess of killing—a dark, destructive goddess—but not of hunting.

In simpler societies around the world, we find hunting to be entirely the province of men. So it appears that originally it was primarily a male "job" or "role" to hunt and provide wild game. The evolution of man has been the evolution of the man as a hunter. Man is a warring and killing animal that society has tamed.

Hunting became a sport in ancient times, and was confined to rulers and their nobles, those with the most leisure and wealth—men only. In ancient Egypt, huntsmen were a social class, taking charge of the dogs at their own hunts and those of the nobles, and bringing home the game. Hunting scenes abound on temple walls in ancient Assyria and Babylonia—men only. Falconry was widely known in ancient India and China—men only.

However, as hunting developed in Europe during the Middle Ages from an efficient way of getting meat with the

"Our descendants will think
we're giants."

least effort to a sport based on a strict code of behavior and standards of game conservation, women became famous at the hunt. Princess Frederika of Eisenach was known for her deer-stalking skill. Maria, governess of the Netherlands, could track a stag, kill it with a bow and gut it with the best of them. In France, Diana de Poitiers even hunted boar from the saddle. In England, Elizabeth I was fond of both hunting and hawking.

In America, we have a long tradition of women with guns. The pioneer wife hunted the woods and swamps and deserts when necessary, although she mostly tended the farmstead and children. America is famous for female dead-eye shots such as Annie Oakley and Calamity Jane. Texas tales of women who hunt are legion. Women belong to many hunting clubs today.

The stereotype of hunters being the high-testosterone crowd is just plain false. A woman who can hunt would be welcome on any hunting trip I can think of.

Little Johnny to his teacher:
"Teacher, I don't want to scare you, but my dad said if I don't start getting better grades, someone is going to get a licking."

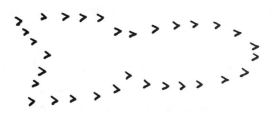

"I think they're pissed."

MYSTERIES

A parachute mind only functions when its open.

Why?

The why? of nature intrigues. Trying to understand and solve problems and mysteries fascinates. I have a long list of whys and hows. Most of us has asked why? all during our lives. Some ask why? and how? defensively, and can hardly wait to move to the next subject, so as to not reveal their personal lack of interest or understanding. Still others ask why and how to show off, knowing full well their audience will be impressed. Showoffs should be handled with a "Tell someone who cares" response. Genuine curiosity, such as a child's, should be given all the attention possible.

It is better to know some of the questions than all of the answers.

As a hunter, I have the following list of curiosities:

Why have I never seen a flock of flying coots migrating south? Do they only fly at night? I have never seen a coot more than thirty feet in the air.

How do salmon and other anadromous fish find their way back to their birth spots? How do fish and marine mammals navigate and communicate in water?

Recently, fishermen started fishing for sockeye salmon in Lake Washington near Seattle with bare colored hooks. Their method proved so successful that others followed, and the game department shortened the season by two weeks because the quota was reached earlier than anticipated.

Why do animals migrate? Food is an obvious reason, but what role does daylight play?

Why are some animals nocturnal?

Why is the lion pride the only social feline group?

Does a bird dog smell the bird's body, feathers or breath?

I have seen bird dogs retrieve with a dead bird in its mouth and point a live bird.

Green hay creates heat. Do chukar and quail eat cheat grass to form a ball of heat in their craw during extreme cold periods? Do Canada geese eat winter wheat grass for the same reason?

Why are matron elk cows the herd leaders? Why does a mare run at the head of wild mustangs?

How does a bird know to build a nest of a particular style, hanging, mud, sticks?

Why does the largest buck of a herd of antelope run at the rear?

Why are most of the male birds the most colorful?

Why do wild sheep go off in bachelor herds?

Do game animals see the ultraviolet spectrum?

The ethmoid bone, which contains a trace of iron, is sensitive to the earth's magnetic field. Can our sense of direction be improved because of this knowledge?

Does the fact that we see something effect what we see?

Why can't hummingbirds walk?

Why does a frog have to close its eyes to swallow?

Why do they call it a camel hair brush when the bristles come from squirrel fur?

Why are all polar bears left handed (pawed)?

How many worms does a robin eat per day?

How many miles does a honeybee travel to collect a pound of honey?

Why is the injury rate per 100,000 hunters only 8.7 and the injury rate per 100,000 baseball players 2,444?

Why has the United States lost 350,000 farms since 1980?

How do they measure the *average* flight speed of a mourning dove?

*"We have no right to assume that any physical laws exist, or
if they have existed up to now, that they will continue to
exist in similar manner in the future."*

Max Planck 1858 -1947
The Universe in the Light of Modern Physics (1931)

*The first day of the 21st century will be
Jan 1, 2001.
The year 2000 still belongs to the 20th century.*

"Three things you can trust...
Old dogs, children and wild turkey."

OPINIONS

There are two sides to every pancake.

Every issue has to sides. It is always wise to listen to both before you make a decision.

Those who oppose hunting have strong opinions, as strong as those of us who believe we have a God-given human right to hunt.

These common factors are used time and again against hunting by the uninformed and animal rights extremists. Some basic responses reply to their arguments.

Anti- "HUNTING IS UNCIVILIZED"
Pro- Hunting is fundamental to man as a toolmaker and a provider. It has been honored as a sport by Pharaohs, Kings and Presidents. Medieval hunting codes were the first conservation laws. Civilization is designed to accommodate many ways of life in an orderly manner. Hunting has its place in any civilization.

Anti- "HUNTING IS MURDER"
Pro- Murder is for one human being to kill another human being unlawfully and with premeditated malice. If it isn't human, it isn't murder—by definition.

Anti- "HUNTERS KILL OTHER HUNTERS"
Pro- Hunting is among the safest of the outdoor sports.

Anti- "HUNTING IS A MACHO THING"
Pro- Macho is the Spanish word for "male." I find no fault in being a self-reliant male capable of defending mysefl.. In the pejorative sense of "aggressively virile," yes, hunting can be a macho thing. Women may participate on equal footing, and many do.

Anti-   "HUNTING PRODUCES AGGRESSION"

Pro-   A questionable assertion no more provable than
         its opposite, "aggression produces hunting."
         Even if it were true, aggression is not all bad.
         If controlled it can be sublimated into com-
         petitiveness, drive and enthusiasm. Hunting
         may also be a release for pent up aggression
         and aggressive behavior.

Anti-   "HUNTING NEGATIVELY EFFECTS WILD-
         LIFE"

Pro-   Hunters hunt and or shoot two types of ani-
         mals, game animals and nuisance or predator
         animals. Certain non-game animals are pro-
         tected. Those who kill non-game or protected
         animals are poachers, not hunters.

                 Hunters only hunt the surplus of the
         game species. That amount has been deter-
         mined by our game departments annually.

                 Hunter related dollars pay for over
         ninety percent of all our states' wildlife depart-
         ments' management of all wildlife, game and
         non-game species.

*Some men haved lived long and lived little, for living is not
measured by length but by use.*

POACHING

Yes, I'm a little bit pregnant.

This is probably the toughest chapter for me to write. My hunting buddies will probably get their biggest laugh if I don't admit to my deeds of poaching. Maybe the statutes of limitation have passed.

In my defense, I hope I've put more back into wildlife than I've taken out.

I've only been caught twice. That means I've only been fined twice.

The first time, I was flat guilty. No excuses. It was January first and I had not bought a new hunting license. I had decided to go hunting at the last minute rather than celebrate the evening before. I was duck hunting alone in flooded pastures near the town of Redmond, Washington. You can't hunt within ten miles of that area today because of the population explosion. Sure enough, here comes a game warden wading out to check me. I tried to talk him into letting me leave my decoys in the pond while I ran into town to get my license. He was pretty narrow-minded on the subject, so I had to pick 'em up.

The second time, I wasn't guilty. I was on our annual goose and duck hunting trip to Northern Alberta. We had hired a guide who had a suspicious background. We didn't know it at the time, but the Federales were out to get him. As such, they followed and observed our every step and action. The evening after the second day's hunt, we were stopped at a roadblock as we headed back to the motel at High Level. It became apparent that they were after any infraction they could add to our "poaching."

There were seven of us altogether counting our guide. During the day we had changed fields from a morning to an afternoon hunt. When we left the first location we left our birds near the blinds for the guide to take to "cleaning lady" that evening. She charged $4.00 per bird and we normally took home over a hundred birds. Most of the birds, both geese and ducks, were immature. At this time of year, September, they were usually full of pinfeathers and not fully feathered out. It made identification of pintails difficult. After two days we had fourteen "pins" which was our possession limit (one pintail per day). The Federales charged the guide with abandoning the birds from the second day and the group with excessive pintails (they claimed we took more than seven on the second day). They tried their hardest to find other infractions but found none. It's surprising, because the way most game laws are written it's hard to not find some minor infraction.

We had flown up in Joe Lane's plane. Joe and Fran are two of my dearest friends. Joe is one of those guys who is going to win. You probably heard the line, "He who dies with the most toys wins." That's Joe. He knows how to play. And he knows how to eat and cook. He had preprepared a special stew that we were ready to sit down and eat when ten Federales knocked on the motel door. They said, "We can talk in our room" or "at the police station." Joe told them that we'd talk when we finished eating. That was not an acceptable alternative. Joe had told all of us that he would be the spokesman for the group because his plane might be at risk. As it turned out, this was not our best option. Joe asked, "What is this all about?" and just about came to blows with an officer who didn't have good chemistry with Joe. The next thing we knew, we were all under arrest and headed for jail. One of the officers was a woman. I just about made a comment about how flat chested she was, but later learned that she was wearing a flack jacket. At the station we were booked, allowed to call an attorney and each had a statement taken. I asked the arresting officer who did not read me my rights to do so, and said that I immediately wanted to contact my attorney. He said I could do so "at the station." He was the same person that had staked us out, so I also asked him if he saw me shoot a pintail. He said he did not see me shoot a pintail. I made him write his statement on the citation. He said we were being cited "as a group." Our attorney missed our court date to plead our "not guilty" position. Our guide was tried separately and fled town. We were fined two-hundred Canadian dollars each, about a hundred sixty real money. Needless to say, we'll never hunt in that "gawd-damn" Alberta again.

You cannot teach a crab to walk straight.

I know this guy who ended the goose season with only minutes left with a five for five shooting demonstration second only to Annie Oakley. It seems these two goose-hunting friends had been out hunting on a new piece of ground that had not been scouted, but was supposed to hold geese. After hunting all day, never firing a shot, the hunting buddies headed back to a cabin near the Columbia River, just before closing time. As they neared the ridge by the river, they saw about two hundred big river geese feeding in a snow-covered field.

"Who owns that piece of land?" asked one of the hunters to the driver.

"I do," came the reply. "Want to shoot them?"

"Hell yes." Didn't take him long to answer.

"Well, I can drop you off beyond that ridge, then come back and start walking toward you. The geese rest in that reserve on the river, and they should fly right over you.

The hunter who was dropped off had a white snow sheet which he covered himself with. He had hunted enough geese to know that they follow their leaders and to not shoot the first birds that flew over.

As the lofter started walking toward the geese, as predicted, the birds easily lifted and started in a long line toward the river, right over the hunter.

Birds started dropping from the sky. One, two, three. All-right, nice shooting — a limit to end the season. Four? Five? I'd sure like to know who that sheeted man was.

The best liar is the one who makes the smallest amount of lying go the furthest.

"Game warden said I was going to roast in hell."

RECIPES

Antelope Liver & Bacon, smothered with onions.

I like to cook and I like to eat good food. During my wandering-star years, I took a job for the hunting season as cook, manager and guide at the Snake River Goose Camp thirty miles northeast of Pasco, Washington.

Mike Bernsen owns Eagle Lake Ranch the company that used to operate the Goose Camp in the heart of the Pacific Coast flyway. Mike's dad, Paul Bernson, and I have been friends for years. The Goose Camp was created by Paul, who I call "Gawdfather"—who also likes to cook. Paul doesn't like eggs, which he refers to as "chicken embryo." He doesn't like where they come from, won't eat them and certainly won't serve them. Paul has also spent a number of years cooking at the camp, much to the consternation of camp guests who like eggs and egg dishes.

Goose hunting was restricted to Saturday, Sunday and Wednesdays, so I had a lot of time to read from the collection of hunting and fishing books Paul had accumulated. Paul is also an accomplished author of a number of outdoor-related books, including a best seller, *The North American Waterfowler.*

George Herter, the same as the outdoor company, was a friend of Paul's, and has written a series of books. He has a couple of books that I became enamored with: *Bull Cook and Authentic Historical Recipes and Practices,* a cookbook that mixes the history of a particular recipe with its instructions. He also blends in celebrities who add a special flavor to his style of writing.

One of my favorite recipes was one that showed the way Ernest Hemingway liked onions and omelets. I experimented with variations and came up with my personal version. I call it a "Snake River Goose Camp Omelet." When I lived in Bend, Oregon, I revised it for a cookbook that was published by the High

Desert Museum as a Desert Omelet in a recipe book called *Seasoned with Sage.* If you want to throw a party for your mouth, try this omelet.

SNAKE RIVER GOOSE CAMP OMELET

1 Kielbasa sausage
Butter for browning
1 clove garlic, crushed or sliced
1/3 to 1/2 large sweet onion, diced (Walla Walla preferred)
1/4 boiled potato, diced
1/4 medium red pepper, diced
1/4 medium green pepper, diced
3 large eggs
Milk, a tip or two
Salt, a dash
Pepper, freshly ground, a couple grinds or more
Picante sauce or freshly made salsa (Your choice of hotness)
Pita Pocket bread (optional)

Cut the Kielbasa into 1/2" angled pieces and cook. I like to put part in the omelet and use the other as a side dish.

Heat enough butter for browning. Do not burn the butter. Add garlic, onion, potato, red and green peppers to butter, sauté quickly.

In a mixing bowl, lightly beat eggs, milk, salt and pepper. Add sautéed vegetables and some of the Kielbasa. Cook in a buttered omelet pan 2 to 3 minutes to desired consistency. Fold omelet and serve with a covering of picante or salsa; or cut pitabread in halves and insert 1/2 omelet in each half, then cover with picante or salsa.

Color may be added by using a sprig of parsley or long slivers of red and green peppers.

This omelet goes well with a side of additional potatoes, onions, peppers, Kielbasa, dark rye toast, raspberry jam and freshly brewed coffee.

I suggest the above ingredients per omelet, per hunter. This is a big serving and can be split to feed two. To feed more, simply repeat and multiply the portions. This is what I call good camp food.

Food is an edible substance occasionally found in reducing diets.

FRYING PAN STEAK

There is only one way to cook a steak and that is fried from a cast iron frying pan.

Start with rendered beef suet. Use enough to cover the bottom of the pan. Do not use butter. Butter burns easily and you need grease hot enough so that it sizzles if you drop a drop of water in it.

I like to butcher my own meat and will buy whole loins to cut 1" to 1 1/4" New York Steak cuts. I like to trim most of the fat so that I have a clean piece of meat. I then lightly salt and heavily pepper each side. Salt and pepper should be applied prior to cooking. They are great simple seasonings and work best when cooked into the meat. Quickly sear each side to hold the juices, then cook until you personally like it. Remove the steak and place on a paper towel allowing the grease from each side ten to fifteen seconds to absorb into the paper. Then, using a quarter inch cube of butter, paint the top of the steak. Quickly remove to warmed or hot plate and serve. It is also essential to serve venison on a hot plate and eat quickly. The tallow in venison becomes distasteful as it cools. If you find a better way to eat steak, please send me the recipe.

MOTHER MUNSON'S BEAN JUICE
& SALAD DRESSING

Jo Ann Munson, a mother I adopted, got me started on a great recipe that works equally well with salads or legumes. I believe it may be the healthiest mix ever - given the medicinal benefits of each of the ingredients..

1 - 8 oz. bottle Gourmet (seasoned) Rice Vinegar
4 heaping tablespoons chopped garlic
4 tablespoons of honey
4 tablespoons extra virgin olive oil

Blend together by shaking before every use. Mother Munson uses an old Dash bottle with large sprinkle holes and a cap as a container. Sprinkle over individual bowls of tossed greens, lettuce, spinach, chopped onion, cauliflower, chopped carrots and tomatoes.

Added zest can be created with crumbled Feta cheese and Greek olives for salads.

When used as a bean juice marinade, I add everything including the complete variety of beans: including garbanzo and red kidney as well as onions, tomatoes, cauliflower, zucchini and cucumbers. You can continue to use the juice by replacing vegetables as you use them.

You can never use too much garlic.

All the hunters in bull camp agreed that there would be no complaining about the cooking, and should there be any, the complainer would become the cook. No one wanted to be cook because it took away from valuable hunting time.

Old Jake had been cook too long. So one day while hunting, he decided to pick up a few elk droppings and spike the stew.

That evening after a hard day's hunt, the hunters returned to a hot meal of "Mountain Man Stew" (not realizing the stew had been spiced).

Digging in, Joe suddenly spit out a dropping, proclaiming. "Elk shit!," then, not missing a beat, followed up with, "Good though."

Only a fool argues with a skunk, a mule or a cook.

Venison liver—deer, elk or moose—has always been a tradition on any hunt. I like to cool it by putting it directly on ice overnight. The next evening's meal is much anticipated because I love liver and bacon smothered in onions.

We were hunting antelope near Buffalo, Wyoming, and had killed a nice buck. I also love to hunt antelope. It's like an American safari. You get to ride around all day, spotting up to five hundred antelope, looking for the big one. Then, if you're lucky enough to hunt the property he's on, there's a great stalk ahead.

I'm not a real fan of antelope meat. I think of most antelope as stinky goats. But with meticulous care their meat is palatable. So, when we gutted the antelope and came to the liver, I decided to give it a try. The next evening I began to wonder about my decision. The antelope smell was as strong as any spoiled piece of meat I've ever smelled. I knew that the majority of their diet was silver-tipped sagebrush. It was later explained to me that the liver is the antelope's filter, so I guess I shouldn't have been that surprised. I did everything right, a half pound of bacon and three large Walla Walla sweets, flour, salt and lots of course black pepper.

It was probably the low point of my cooking career. I could not finish the first bite. What a waste of bacon and onions.

I didn't say the meat was tough,
I said I couldn't cut the gravy.

AN APPLE A DAY KEEPS THE DOCTOR AWAY.

It's the truth. An apple is a miracle food as well as being one of the most stubborn fruits grown. No scientist has ever been able to duplicate a selected apple variety from its seed. Grafting is the only way a grower can reproduce a particular variety such as Jonathans or Red Delicious. Plant a Macintosh seed and you get a primitive apple that doesn't resemble a Macintosh.

The secrets about apples have been known for over 2,000 years. They were confirmed in 1962, when 1,381 students from Michigan State took part in a test by eating an apple a day for two quarters. Records were kept and compared with 17,000 other students. The results showed without doubt that students who ate apples daily had far less of the two most frequent illnesses — colds and nervous disorders. They had a far better health record for all other diseases. Similar tests were held in Belgian and German Universities with the same conclusions.

There is a long history of apples being used in the Mediterranean countries and Scandinavia to cure nervous disorders as well as improving one's general health.

Apple cider has been used for the same purposes. Apple vinegar was also used in Europe as a tranquilizer for nervous disorders and alcoholics. For a healthy life take an apple a day, a cup of cider or three teaspoons of apple vinegar.

WILD RICE WILD FOWL STUFFING

Using a three quart pot, bring three cups of cold water to a boil then add three cubes of bouillon and one cup of washed wild rice and cook for ten minutes. Then cook for an additional fifty minutes at a slightly lower heat than boiling or until most of the wetness is removed. Do not let burn. You can pour off the excess if the rice is tender.

In a separate saucepan at medium heat, cut six slices of bacon into half inch pieces until half done, add one tablespoon of butter and one sliced onion. Sauté until half done, then add three bay leaves, one teaspoon of oregano, one and a half cup of chopped celery, and one small can of mushroom bits and pieces. Stir together, blending and heating for two minutes.

Empty saucepan into wild rice, salt and pepper and mix together.

Individually stuff each bird (from chukar to wild turkey) and bake using your preferred method.

This recipe also makes a great main dish by adding one can of cream of mushroom soup then baking the complete mixture for thirty minutes at 325 degrees.

"WALLA WALLA GOBBLER"

Each thanksgiving, or turkey dinner, I can hardly wait for what I believe in the very best sandwich you can make.

Accept no substitutes —

Start with one-quarter inch slices of white breast meat. Take two slices of white bread and butter each side, (do not use butter substitutes). Then spread Miracle Whip dressing (not mayonnaise) generously over the butter. Using only Walla Walla sweet onions, take two one-quarter inch slices and cut to fit flush on one side of the bread. Now cut to fit the turkey to the bread. Salt and pepper with freshly ground coarse pepper. Neatly fit leaf lettuce over meat. Put together, cut into halves and enjoy.

RIGHT TO HUNT

We need a new constitutional amendment.

There is a legal right to hunt.

In his book *The Right to Hunt*, James Biser Whisker eloquently outlines the precedents of our right to hunt.

The law had been misused in ages past to reserve hunting for the few, but overall, hunting rights are the rights of men. As rights broadened generally, so they broadened specifically to permit hunting by most or all men. Even when state power proscribed hunting of some species by commoners, it still permitted hunting of other species by ordinary people.

The state's power to enforce conservation is clearly recognized in civilized nations. Meat and market hunters may violate such laws, but the sport hunter supports them out of self interest. That is the best reason generally for people to support the law. Hunters know that future hunts, not only by themselves, but also by ensuing generations, are guaranteed only when strict conservation is practiced. Thus the hunter will obey and respect hunting laws that limit or close seasons or limit kills.

We conclude that, overall, the state may not properly close public lands entirely to hunting. Certain safety and protective steps, such as requiring a guide to be present, may be taken.

But beyond legality there is the practical side of conservation. Unlimited herds die of starvation in winter. Some herds grow so large beyond their food sources that governments employ and pay professional hunters tax money to kill (and waste) surplus game. This is a compelling practical reason to permit sport hunting. The guides and other costs of sport hunting are borne by individual hunters, not the general public.

Finally, we see the right to hunt possibly protected under the unenumerated rights contained in Amendment IX to the U. S. Constitution. Other unspecified rights are now so protected, and thus hunting may eventually be incorporated and protected. There is substantial evidence suggesting that the Supreme Court of the United States could one day recognize the right to hunt. Presently, the right to hunt may be placed in that category wherein men claim a natural right but the state has yet to take notice of that right. And that makes the right so claimed no less real.

Hunting has proved to be of incidental but substantial value to the state. The 1966 Arthur D. Little Report to The U. S. Army on the National Board to Promote Rifle Practice concluded that shooting sports, hunting included, provide Thai armed forces with a significant reservoir of trained manpower. Such men make better soldiers and are more efficient as soldiers. They shoot better, they fire their weapons in combat more frequently, and they suffer fewer casualties than untrained troops. The United States Supreme Court in 1938 ruled that state's (and, presumably, federal) government may not act in such a way with gun laws as to prevent the maintenance of this reservoir of skilled manpower. Conceivably this reservoir could be filled by hunters, and thus their right would be protected under the Second Amendment to the United States Constitution.

In the final analysis, only the state has power to prevent hunting. Organized religion, theological teaching and ethical considerations may suffice to prevent some from hunting, yet they lack enforcement power. And the democratic state does not ordinarily forbid large numbers of people from an arguably legitimate pursuit.

We plant trees for the benefit of another generation.

SEX

What not to name your dog.

Everybody who has a dog calls him Sam or Rover. I call mine "Sex." Now, Sex has been very embarrassing to me. When I went to City Hall to renew his dog license, I told the clerk I would like to have a license for Sex. He said, "I'd like to have one, too." Then I said, "But this is a dog." He said he didn't care what she looked like. Then I said, "You don't understand, I've had Sex since I was nine years old." He said I must have been quite a kid.

When I got married and went on my honeymoon, I took the dog with me. I told the motel that I wanted a room for my wife and me and a special room for Sex. He said that every room in the place was for sex. I said, "You don't understand, Sex keeps me awake at night." The clerk said, "Me too."

One day I entered Sex in a contest, but before the competition began, the dog ran away. Another contestant asked me why I was just standing there looking around. I told him I had planned to have Sex in the contest. He told me I should have sold tickets. "But, you don't understand, I said. I had hoped to have Sex on TV." He called me a showoff.

When my wife and I separated, we went to court to fight over custody of the dog. I said, "Your Honor, I had Sex before I was married." The judge said, "Me too." When I told him that after I was married, Sex left me. He said, "Me too."

Last night, Sex ran off again. I spent hours looking around town for him. A cop came over to me and asked, "What are you doing in this alley at 4 o'clock in the morning?" I said, "I'm looking for Sex."

My case comes up Friday.

Marriage is a trick of prostitution.

I once named a litter of bird dogs Rolex, Timex, Seiko, Cartier, Longines and Tiffany. I figured that if they didn't turn out to be good bird dogs they would make good watch dogs.

WANTED

A good woman.
Must fish and hunt,
skin and gut,
clean and shovel,
cook and sew.
Must have gun,
horse and saddle.
Please send photo of
gun, horse and saddle.

The only time a woman can change a man is when he's a baby.

"They're making fun of our shooting."

STAGES

The evolution of the hunter.

Recently, two avid hunters and behavioral scientists, Robert Jackson and Robert Norton, undertook a five year project in which they interviewed and observed over 1,000 Wisconsin hunters.

The conclusion was that the best hunters are people who know, understand and love the outdoors and that they progress through phases or stages in their evolution. These people have the insights and a perspective about natural things based upon their "HANK" or "experiencing" — the only true way of knowing. These experiences develop into way of life for many of us. Many lessons learned and accumulated from hunting affect all of our values, relationships and appreciations.

During the Jackson-Norton study many hunters related significant experiences with wildlife and the woods, association with fellow hunters, a unique, shared experience with a son or daughter, a grandson or grand-daughter, and certainly the ambivalent feeling created by the kill. Statistical analysis indicated that patterns of hunter motivation and behavior are strongly influenced by both hunter age and years hunting. Many older hunters said they no longer had the need to fill their game bag. Bagging the limit was no longer everything. When asked the question, "If you had only one more hunting day in your lifetime, how would you spend it?" some hunters seemed to discover through reflection that hunting's satisfactions were now built around a much broader base of experiences. The researchers finally broke hunter phases into five stages:

1) SHOOTER STAGE

The hunter talked about satisfaction of hunting being closely tied to being able to "get shooting." Often the young beginning duck hunter would relate that he had an excellent day of hunting and what was excellent was that he had gotten "a lot of shooting." The novice deer hunter would talk about the number of shooting opportunities, and missing game was of little consequence. The beginning hunter apparently wants to pull the trigger and test out the capability of his weapon.

2) LIMITING-OUT STAGE

The hunter still talked about satisfaction gained from shooting, but what seemed more important was measuring success and self through the killing of game and the number of birds or animals shot. The duck hunter would say: "Had a good day, got four out of five." The deer hunter seemed to enjoy describing a long or running shot, but the absolute measure of the hunt was filling that tag. Most hunters will also recognize this stage in fellow hunters who brag, "Yes, our party filled."

3) TROPHY STAGE

At this stage of development, satisfaction was described in terms of selectivity of game, usually reflecting the hunter's idea of a trophy. The duck hunter might take only green-heads and pass up good shots on birds of less status. The deer hunter, of course, sought the big buck. Shooting opportunity and skills are now of lesser importance. Deer hunters in this phase would pass up a small buck and wait for the big one — even until the next season. They were also willing to travel distances to hunt areas that might produce a really big buck.

4) METHOD STAGE

It is characterized by an intensity or almost religious fervor about hunting. This hunter usually has all of the specialized equipment: decoys, calls, camouflaged boat and retriever. Hunting has become one of the most important dimensions of that person's life. It's what he does best and he lives off the opportunity to practice that expertise. Seldom did satisfaction primarily relate to the "taking of game" at this stage, but instead switched to method. Hunters bagged to hunt, not hunted to bag. Taking of game was necessary and intrinsic, but secondary to "how" it was done. Specialization or handicapping became the prime factor in satisfaction. A duck hunter might talk at length about decoying, the layout, picking a site, wind and weather variables, and the qualities of different kinds of decoys—and then finally describe what it was like to watch as a flock began to "work the blocks." Expert callers told of their special satisfactions in turning a high bird, and then talking it in. In this state the deer hunter now wants to take the white-tail on a "one-on-one" basis or with a selected partner.

5) SPORTSMAN STAGE

Research findings indicate a "mellowing out" stage which apparently many hunters do not reach until about 40 years of age and after many years of hunting experience. At this point, the hunter finds satisfaction in the total hunting experience. The hunter seemed to be fully mature as a person and as a hunter (or is it burned out?). As such, he no longer needed to measure his worth or control his world by the taking of game. Instead he talked of hunter satisfaction in terms of a total appreciation of nature or the companionship of partners or family. He is the duck hunter back at the beginning, satisfied to be afield, to experience the out-of-doors in its completeness, to anticipate and appreciate, and to feel completely satisfied with that experience. Not many talked at this stage, but those that did know who they are.

How does a person get to this stage of oneness with the environment? What are the ingredients? *Time* is certainly one factor. But perhaps certain *unique experiences* provide the second element? Where are you on this scale?

Most of the luxuries and so-called comforts of life are not only unnecessary, but also positive hindrances to the evolution of man.

Time is a stream I go fishing in.

I grow old learning many things.

TERRITORIAL IMPERATIVE

"This is my hunting spot."

Most people protect trade secrets that give them an advantage. In hunting, if you show some dude a good place to hunt, you can probably kiss it good-bye. The next weekend or season he will return with his buddies to the success of the spot you showed him. Many new hunters have not had enough experience to scout and find huntable areas on their own. Sometimes it's hard to find property boundaries. And, of course, easily accessible hunting spots are usually over-run with other hunters. And, while you can't blame them, most eager young hunters abuse and over-hunt new candy stores.

I used to have a couple coveys of California Valley Quail that I could count on for a half dozen birds each year. They were great to train and work the field trial dogs on. After the covey flushed, we could hunt singles and get up to a dozen solid points on our young bird dogs. After showing some friends where they were, their return hunts eliminated the coveys. A guy works hard to find these spots and cherishes them.

A number of animals have strong territorial imperatives, but I don't believe any animal is more protective than man. There are spatial imperatives, where some people don't even like others standing close to them. Most property owners fence their property as much for territorial proof of ownership as for keeping something in or out.

The closest emotion to the territorial imperative is probably jealousy and jealousy is a poison.

The important point to remember is that as humans we have the ability to control our emotions. So the next time you take someone to your secret hunting spot, blindfold them and tell them you're going to shoot them if you ever see them hunting in your spot without your permission.

The illusion that times that were, were better than those that are has probably pervaded all ages.

"That wasn't a miss, J-Boy. Papa Jake just fired a warning shot so this duck hunting wouldn't look too easy."

WISDOM

The art of achieving and hunting.

The chase is the hunt.

Only three everyday events use all of our senses: making love, drinking wine and hunting. The more slowly we use each sense, the more gratification we derive.

To hunt is to live, to learn, to remember and to dream.

"An aphorism never coincides with the truth:
It is either a half-truth or one-and-a-half truths..."
                                        Karl Kraus (1874 - 1936)

These aphorisms serve the hunter and the non-hunter alike.

EVERYTHING HAS ITS SEASON

Eat what is in season. Prepare your eating habits around foods that are fresh and taste best at the peaks of their seasons. There is no better apple than a tree-ripened apple picked from the top of an apple tree you just climbed on a crisp cool morning.

YOU CANNOT DRINK TOO MUCH CLEAN COLD WATER

Water is life to all living things. To drink from a high mountain stream, its water so cold that it hurts, is a rare experience.

THE SUN GENERATES LIFE

Don't waste the morning by getting up late. The sun brings another day of growth and living and provides a kaleidoscope for the eyes.

Use the sun wisely, for it is the light of life and death.

LISTEN, REALLY LISTEN

Sound, at the right time and place is noise, and at the right time and place, music.

Song is the music of life.

Know what you are talking about, and learn when you're listening.

EXERCISE DAILY

Go walkabout.

The hunter was made to walk, not run. The runner cannot enjoy the view or stop to observe and smell the flowers.

Don't live life in a hurry. Take the time to exercise and organize. Size up the task at hand so that it can be accomplished well, with style, in a timely and pleasurable manner.

GOD IS A VERB

The inner spirit of the hunter is as important as his intellect and physical body.

Choose a faith that calms and gives meaning and purpose. Then, keep a happy ending in mind.

KNOW YOURSELF

Be true to yourself. Be strong enough to do the thing that is right when no one else is looking.

An intelligent man thinks about everything, knowing that much is hidden that he will never know.

Do not let anyone discover the limits of your capabilities.

Never talk about yourself.

Class requires style, but style doesn't make class.

Trust your heart, but do nothing in the heat of passion.

KNOWLEDGE IS LONG

Life is short.

The more a hunter uses his senses, the better armed he is.

Greatness requires an imaginative mind, a deep comprehension, a cultured taste and clear thinking.

KNOW YOUR FRIENDS AND YOUR ENEMIES

Make teachers of both your friends and enemies.

Since one is known by the friends he keeps, the best way to have hunting friends is to make them. Find hunters who will help shoulder your misfortunes and you will never be alone. Blend their friendship with conversation of tradition, learning and understanding. Cherish them as you would your family, for they are a part of you.

Always keep your enemies in front of you and your friends in back of you.

In gambling, you do not play the card your opponent expects or needs.

LUCK IS AN ART

There are rules to luck. A studied situation can be more predictable than an unstudied one. Therefore, one can manipulate his own good fortune or luck.

Bad luck is usually the excuse of losers. Betting on long odds is the game of fools.

The harder you hunt smart, the luckier you get.

LESS IS MORE

It is all a matter of priorities: time spent working indoors or time spent outdoors, climbing stairs or climbing mountains, crossing streets or crossing streams.

Much that brings pleasure is not owned.

In everything, that which is least expected is most esteemed.

No two hunts are alike. Each is unique, filled with anticipation. All hunting is precious, scant in quantity and high in quality.

We can only take pleasure from time. So, enjoy a little more and strive a little less. For no matter what little we can add to this lifetime, it will take nothing away for the amount of time we spend later.

SMILE, YOU'RE HUNTING

Happiness isn't something you experience.

It's something you remember. Happiness, health, laughter and joy follow a smiling face. A smile is a language that even a baby understands.

The happiest people seem to be those who have no particular reason for being happy except that they are.

CHASE RAINBOWS

Every man is a hero to his imagination. It is comfort to remember that if our dreams haven't come true, neither have our nightmares.

The longer you live, the less importance you attach to things, and the less importance you also attach to importance.

Truth is stranger than fiction, and harder to make up.

ASSUME YOU'RE WRONG, THEN PROVE YOU'RE RIGHT

The simplest words, Yes and No, take the most thought. Measure twice, cut once. Believe only yourself. For a moment, a lie is the truth.

LASTING IMPRESSIONS

There is only one chance to make a good first or last impression. In between, you're are earning your reputation. Be honest and never make excuses. Never exaggerate or use superlatives: they offend the truth and can ruin your reputation for good taste, integrity and judgment. If you are complimented for a job well done, there is only one response.

"Thank You."

It is characteristic of wisdom not to do desperate things.

"I don't know if I can go... I've got a migrating headache."

YOUTH

You can't whip a colt for being a colt.

While deer hunting in Georgia, I came upon a young boy hiding behind a tree, looking up into the air. I must have startled him because he jumped straight up when I spoke to him. On the other side of the tree was a pile of squirrels. There must have be fifteen or twenty, maybe more.

I explained I wasn't the game warden and that he didn't have anything to worry about. And it would be OK for his friend to come out. He said he was alone, but I figured that one boy couldn't have shot that many squirrels.

"Where's your gun?" I inquired.

"Got none." replied the boy.

Now, I knew for some reason that the boy was lying.

"How did you kill them squirrel then, huh?"

"This here smooth rock." answered the boy.

Then all of a sudden we heard a rustle high up in the tree and the boy instinctively whipped off the rock, which struck the squirrel in the head. We walked over to pick up his stone dead squirrel.

"Well, I'll be. I never saw such a feat," I said. "You just might be the best left-hander I ever saw."

"Ain't left-handed." said the boy, a little indignant.

"Now son, you don't have to lie to me." (I thought he might be one of those habitual liars.) "I saw you throw that stone left-handed."

"Ain't left-handed!" the boy snapped back. "I'm right-handed."

It didn't make no sense to me. I used to pitch when I was younger and knew a good thrower when I saw one.

"Well, if you're right handed, how come you throw left handed?

"Papa made me throw left handed," he said. "Throwing right handed I tore 'em up too bad."

Youth is totally experimental.

"They're young. They'll turn around."

EPILOGUE

Why we hunt is very personal and often difficult to answer. I hope this book has helped in your understanding of the heritage and traditions of hunting and provided you with some answers for yourself and others about hunting. I hope you may have had a chuckle or two while I was having fun.

And should you continue to pursue hunting, take a young one with you on your next hunting trip. Let them determine for themselves what hunting is all about, and whether or not they want to make hunting a part of their lives.

You'll always stay young if you eat properly, sleep sufficiently, exercise daily — and lie about your age.

QUANTITY DISCOUNTS
Politically Correct Hunting

Give a copy to everyone you know!

Now is the time to get this book into the hands of every American. Order 25, 50, or 100 copies. Send them to your friends. Give them to business associates. Mail one to everyone you know.

DISCOUNT SCHEDULE

1 copy	$14.95	25 copies	$250.00
5 copies	$67.00	50 copies	$425.00
10 copies	$120.00	100 copies	$800.00
	500 copies	$3,750.00	

ORDER YOURS TODAY!
Call (206) 454-7009 or use the coupon below

Merril Press
P.O. Box 1682
Bellevue, WA 98009

Please send me _____ copies of **Politically Correct Hunting**. Enclosed is a check or money order in the amount of $_____.
Please charge my: ☐ VISA ☐ MasterCard
Card Number_____
Expires _____
Print Name_____
Street_____
City_____
State_____ZIP_____
Phone (_____)_____